FINANCIAL Epiphany

Discover Your Ability to Multiply Money and Reimagine Your Financial Life

SCOTT YAMAMURA

www.createdtocreate.com

ISBN: 979-8-9913857-0-1 (paperback)
ISBN: 979-8-9913857-1-8 (ebook)

Library of Congress Control Number: 2024919891

Ordering Information:
Special discounts are available on quantity purchases by corporations, associations, and others. For details, contact scott@financialepiphany.com

Publisher's Cataloging-in-Publication Data
Names: Yamamura, Scott, 1975- .
Title: Financial epiphany : discover your ability to multiply money and reimagine your financial life / Scott Yamamura.
Description: Bellevue, WA : Created to Create, 2025. | Includes 33 b&w charts. | Summary: Provides a simple, unconventional three-step solution to investing, helping individuals understand the multiplying power they wield with money at various ages in their life. Understanding this can lead to making positive changes with money and taking confident action for investing for the future.
Identifiers: LCCN X | ISBN 9798991385701 (pbk) | ISBN 9798991385718 (ebook)
Subjects: LCSH: Finance, Personal. | Finance, Personal – United States. | Investments. | Saving and investment. | BISAC: BUSINESS & ECONOMICS / Personal Finance / General. | BUSINESS & ECONOMICS / Personal Finance / Money Management. | BUSINESS & ECONOMICS / Personal Finance / Investing.
Classification: LCC HG179.Y36 2025 | DDC 332.024 Y--dc23
LC record available at https://lccn.loc.gov/X

To Dad for showing me how to seek unconventional solutions, and to Mom for demonstrating that saving money can be a natural and seamless behavior.

To my wife, Su, and son, Logan, for walking alongside as we put these financial ideas into practice.

And to all you readers who plan to make a difference in your financial lives.

CONTENTS

APPENDIXES: THE DETAILS THAT HELP KEEP THE REST OF THE BOOK SIMPLE

CHAPTER 1

Preparing Ourselves to Think Differently

A mental miracle, an eye-opening experience, a sudden and enlightening realization. An epiphany. These are the kinds of moments that drop us to our knees, causing us to throw our arms up toward the sky as we experience overcoming a long-time barrier. If you've ever suddenly received clarity on a solution to a problem you've been mulling over for some time, you might have had an epiphany—an insight that brought great understanding to the issue at hand. It can feel like fireworks. Your mind feels electric.

How would conquering something as intimidating and overwhelming as money feel—having an aha moment about your funds? I'm not talking about getting on the same level of understanding as a stockbroker, and I'm not alluding to achieving accountant, banker, or financial advisor levels of know-how about money. I'm talking about *you*. You as you are. You arriving at an understanding of one of the most uncanny phenomena money has to offer—how to multiply your money—and how that single understanding can be the breakthrough you've been waiting for.

But you see, we have a problem that stands in our way. Let's just name it. To put it plainly, we overspend and we undersave. And when I say *we*, I'm not just talking about you and me—I'm talking about the whole nation and beyond. We've always known we should be properly tending to the money we oversee—we just haven't been able to get ourselves to do it with any gusto yet. We struggle in a tug-of-war relationship between spending and saving. We know better, but do we do better?

Think of a parent allowing their child to run about their day unattended and unstructured, with no expectation to attend school, do homework, participate in chores, or recognize a bedtime. Without a purpose assigned to their waking hours, the child's days could easily devolve into an all-day every day routine of consumption of entertainment and occupying a couch. Do you love that child? Provide them with structure.

Likewise, we must assign a purpose to our money. Without purpose, money tends to find its own less productive activities to engage in. Money does not like to sit still. It's an active tool. And if we do not assign it a big enough purpose, it will likely walk off and find a way to be spent unnecessarily.

So, we need a why. We need a why that is so big it will quell our conspicuous consumption. It needs to be something so significant that our other behaviors would willingly submit to and orbit around it. Together, we will discover this why and explore how to unleash it as one of our greatest capabilities. It's a superpower of sorts that remains largely untapped, waiting for us to take confident action on it.

And just what is this superpower we harbor? It is our ability to increase, proliferate, and multiply money—to grow money upon itself, then upon itself, and upon itself again. Financially, the results can be staggering. We are the stewards, and we must be responsible with our power as we invite our own 800-pound gorilla to be released to pound our financial behaviors into order.

Each of us is born with this money-multiplying superpower, but most of us only timidly call upon it across our lifetimes. We sit on our hands. And why? No one has truly helped us feel aware of this power we wield. We're all born with it. We all possess it. But we treat it like a sidenote, relegated to a place on the bench apart from matters we've allowed to be more pressing.

In this book, we'll work to understand this power of ours so we can finally comprehend it for what it is and choose to apply it with decisive action and the conviction it deserves. Over these pages, we will become equipped. We will become empowered. By realizing this profound superpower we all command, we can take ownership of our finances and begin confidently multiplying them. And, as a result, our spending can deprioritize, finally and naturally falling back into the place it deserves to be.

So, all we need is a spark. Something to ignite this change in us. Something so delightfully unconventional yet uncomplicated that it just works.

THE ORIGINS OF THIS EPIPHANY

I always wondered how my father, George, could come up with the strikingly unique solutions he did. He earned international attention by leading his aerospace team at Boeing to become one of the first three organizations in the world to be recognized as a level five operation, a measure of excellence in technology. The honor was bestowed by the Software Engineering Institute, a federally funded research and development center at Carnegie Mellon

University. Witnessing my father receive this prestigious rating for developing spacecraft software helped me gain an appreciation for his unprecedented processes. He had been modeling them for me my whole life. It's natural to doubt our parents, but maybe my father was really onto something after all.

He traveled the world, speaking to companies that wanted to learn more about his approaches, and was commissioned by his employer to write a book, titled *The 10th Inning*, to pass down his unique perspective to others. Of the many ways he could have themed his book, he chose to share his most highly regarded aerospace principles by using stories from his time as a Little League baseball coach—while the typical baseball game consists of nine innings, this 10th inning concept referred to applying strategies beyond regular gameplay, continuing them into work life. And it was just like my dad to do that, to think of what the reader needed. He could have gone technical. He could have gone niche, jotting down jargon and complexities. But, as always, he stayed true to his principles and valued his audience first. Simplifying. Inviting all to succeed.

As he recounted in his book, my brother and I were the leftovers—the ones without jerseys who wouldn't have been able to play T-ball unless my dad volunteered to form a team. He was a first-timer as a coach, and we were first-timers as young players. Our kickoff game would be the true litmus test of what our early team practices were amounting to. And all too soon that initial game did arrive.

Our first batter was up. He smacked the ball off of the tee and ran the wrong direction, straight to third base! "No, no," my dad yelled. "Come back, come back. Not third base! You need to run to first base!"

Well, our batter ended up having enough time to run back and safely arrive at first—because the other team was still trying to make the play at third!

The next batter was up, and his swing sent a grounder toward first base. Our runner at first stepped off the base, picked up the ball, and threw it to first, getting himself and his teammate out. And the other team didn't even have to touch the ball!

"Pick up the ball, tag the runner, throw to first, step on the base…no, not that base!" yelled parents and coaches from both sides.

I've realized managing our money is just like walking onto a baseball field at age six. So many things to know and so many competing voices. Pay off your house, don't pay off your house. This is good debt—no, it's bad debt. Build up your credit score, cut up your credit cards.

Many of us have been told to invest our money, but what's the result going to be? The popular answer is "I don't know." How can we get excited about "I don't know"? We're like six-year-old baseball players, running every which way on the field in the wrong direction, letting others make our decisions for us.

> Cashier: "Hello, would you like to save 25% with us today?"
> Us: "Sure."
>
> Salesman: "Hello, can I interest you in upgrading to our platinum model?"
> Us: "That sounds good."
>
> Credit card representative: "Hello. You get a free T-shirt if you sign up for our credit card today."
> Us: "Do you have a medium?"

My father so astutely observed that kids at the age of six couldn't actually comprehend all the intricate and nuanced rules that determine America's favorite pastime. So, he did an amazing thing—he started simplifying.

The idea was not to expect a motley bunch of untrained children to understand the constantly shifting game of baseball from the get-go. He knew our six-year-old minds weren't ready to make the necessary decisions on the fly under pressure, so he unraveled and reassembled strategies to make them age appropriate.

My dad trained us with a distinctive technique while we were on defense. To get an out, we had to both step on the needed base *and* tag the runner. Only one is required in the game, but if we did both, we always got the out, no matter which move was required in the moment. As unorthodox as this was, it got the required results consistently. Parents no longer yelled out for us to do one thing or the other, because we were already covering both possible options. This sent out a "wow" among the crowd and gave us a leg up.

In furthering these unique approaches, when fielding, Dad trained us to get the ball only to the designated base we were positioned by. Each player in the field only needed to remember a single base to throw to. This removed errors that came from making poor decisions or inaccurately throwing the ball to far-off bases.

Gone were the times of the ball chaotically being tossed about the field, as each player instead threw immediately and confidently to a predetermined baseman. To the unsuspecting onlooker, the team appeared to magically improve at throwing, catching, and halting runners. Players improved rapidly as my father mounted up simplified methods across all aspects of gameplay.

Coaching six-year-olds playing baseball and empowering folks with personal finance have a lot in common. Both are appropriately intimidating topics for their groups. The sort of simple, every-time plan my father employed removed complexities for the players and caused us to make more outs, win more games, and take home championship trophies seven years in a row between my brother and me. In addition, team morale and confidence soared. Something was working, consistently. Coach Dad's solutions, which defied conventional wisdom, were solving the problem at hand.

After witnessing my dad develop remarkable solutions in seemingly unrelated areas of life, including his aerospace career, kids' sports, and beyond, I started to look for my own simpler solutions as well. Maybe witnessing him throughout my life gave me the bug to identify common problems and seek out novel ways to go about dealing with them. Consider the realm of personal finance—with so many of us financially struggling, it qualifies as a field ripe for the application of novel solutions.

For many years of my life, I've been a family man who worked a corporate job. I love how common that is. There are a few things that have been intimidating for me over the years: handling personal finances, understanding how to maintain a car, and taking care of a house. I love how normal those issues are. Upon sheepishly tip-toeing myself into the world of personal finance, I unexpectedly found myself developing a voracious appetite for learning about money via books, workshops, online materials, and more for years on end. Once I was inside the gates, I found that comprehending money maybe wasn't so bad after all. Upon closer inspection, money actually looked more like a sheep masquerading in wolf's clothing, less threatening than its reputation claimed.

Once I had been immersed in the subject long enough, I zealously met with three different financial advisors within two weeks of each other just to go over my finances and discuss their varied approaches. That daring feat was something I never would have ventured into before finding my newfound financial confidence. I even took a deeper dive, studying to be certified as a financial coach, just so I could immerse myself in the many financial matters relevant to the everyday person. Overcoming my own barriers with my money thoughts taught me that if we can find confidence where we previously lacked it, it can free us up to make great strides.

An obsession. That's what my wife, Su, has been calling it. But amid this hunger to understand money, I stumbled upon a way of thinking about it that suddenly clicked, creating an unquenchable excitement. I experienced an epiphany, and it flipped the script on how I saw money, bringing into focus a picture that differed from the world's way of teaching it. And by looking from this new vantage point, I realized this view could be shared with others and change more lives than just my own.

This simple way of thinking has worked wonders for my family, as it motivated us to pay off hundreds of thousands of dollars in debt. This freed us up to hit milestones and complete goals ahead of time regarding retirement, college savings, and more. Each time we crossed a finish line within one area of finance, the momentum carried us to swiftly start the next fund to cover things like financing home business costs, facilitating giving, and helping other generations of the family. These possibilities opened up after I finally grasped our ability to multiply money.

Only a fraction of us are financially healthy. Most of us are not. I see you there, and if you're like the rest of us you've likely got debts to pay and money that needs to be better managed. But what if we can move the needle so you and the next slice of folks can make a change? There's so much power that's been right under our noses this whole time, and so many of us are poised to take advantage of it. And that's why I'm sharing this with you. Because normal, everyday people can benefit from this way of understanding money. Your finances can grow to new heights and be put toward a new purpose. You can do this—and you can do it just as you are.

THE EPIPHANY THAT SAVED A FAMILY AND INSPIRED THE WORLD

William Kamkwamba was a 14-year-old Malawian boy expelled from school because his family could not afford his school fees. His story could have taken a continuous downward trajectory from there. But instead, young Kamkwamba practiced a dose of righteous rebellion by sneaking back into the school library to keep learning. During this time, his family's farm and the greater country of Malawi were suffering from a punishing season of drought, resulting in hunger and running the people thin on hope.

In this time of struggle, Kamkwamba discovered a particular book in the school library called *Using Energy* explaining the science behind windmills. He selected and held steadfast to the idea of a windmill as the breakthrough to the famine his family was facing. He tenaciously studied from books, salvaged materials from the junkyard, and pushed for a wind-powered answer to the long dry spell.

One day, during a phase of pondering and reflection, he became fixated on the wheel of a bicycle. As he observed the wheel spinning, he noticed how it created power for the safety light of the bicycle. He was witnessing the workings of a device attached to the bike known as a dynamo, which converts mechanical movement to electricity. Like this bicycle wheel, a windmill could operate in a similar fashion with the wind revolving the blades to generate power. This power could, in turn, pump water from underground to quench crops.

In Kamkwamba's mind, previously unrelated pieces of information came together. The bicycle wheel and windmill overlapped in his mind. After his previous phase of struggle, his brain was hungry and his eyes were primed to recognize a unique solution once it was ready to present itself. The connection was made in his mind. He experienced a moment of epiphany that set him off even more boldly in his determination to build a wind-powered structure.

After encountering resistance from his father who saw his plight and use of time as squandering, he constructed a windmill against great odds. That windmill generated electricity and pumped water to provide irrigation. His family and farm were saved.

This story emphasizes the benefit of focusing intently on a single solution. Kamkwamba discovered a single vision of a windmill that energized him along a bold mission he was bound to accomplish. If we break down his story, we can perceive the four steps that make up the process of experiencing an epiphany.

Step 1: Seeking a Solution

William Kamkwamba snuck into his library, read, researched, and built a field of understanding around his selected remedy: windmills.

Step 2: The Struggle

Kamkwamba experienced two headwinds to building a windmill. One was the drought, which brought ongoing hunger and strife. The other was fighting for time and resources to experiment with solutions despite a lack of support from others. He continued to look for an answer amid this adversity.

Step 3: Coming to a Realization

Kamkwamba came to understand that a bicycle wheel powering a safety light could parallel the design of a windmill that powers a water pump. Patterns between the two systems emerged that had been previously undetected.

Step 4: Taking Action

Kamkwamba built his windmill and proceeded to live a life of inspiration and purpose. The windmill not only brought answers for his family, but its impacts rippled across his village, his country, and, finally, the world.

William Kamkwamba now continues his quest to help communities through his organization, the Moving Windmills Project. His determination and perseverance are inspirational on an international scale for those seeking renewable energy solutions for rural and underserved communities. The ingenuity he exercised alone is celebrated.

What's so welcoming about his story is we can walk through the very same phases he did to increase the likelihood of experiencing a new realization in our own lives. We can follow his blueprint. The next sections of this book are grouped into the very same steps we just discussed: Seeking a Solution, The Struggle, Coming to a Realization, and Taking Action.

Kamkwamba experienced a realization that helped him overcome the effects of poverty, drought, lack of resources, engineering challenges, and more to unwaveringly assemble a windmill that blew his challenges away. Do we desire that kind of electric experience with our finances? The kind strong enough to rewire how we use money? To leave such an impression that it can change how we live—behavior, thoughts, and all?

The journey to realizing an epiphany is a process, and it will take some patience to work through these pages to build up to having a discovery of our own. After all, the world has been teaching us one way of doing things, so we'll need to spend some pages retraining our minds to think differently. Multiplying money is one of the most powerful opportunities we'll ever have. And with a lifetime of work and earnings to steward, it's well worth building the proper foundation here to release it into our lives.

Some of the words to come will hopefully stimulate your mind with new thoughts. And some words of tough love may carry a little sting. But this is all part of readying our minds to accept a new idea as we both expose and reject any unhealthy habits that have been blocking us. These words here are written for you, so you don't have to expect to engage in heavy amounts of toil over money to discover your own personal epiphany. The fact that you picked up this book is putting you in the direct line of sight of one.

STEP 1

Seeking a Solution

Committing to a journey that is challenging but worth it.

Chapters:

CHAPTER 2

You're Not an Impostor—This Is Possible

The first step in our journey is the Seeking a Solution stage. We'll start by dismantling an all-too-common obstacle in order to clear the path for our minds to rethink money. If we are to truly see multiplying money for what it is, we must first dispel any myths that are sending us astray.

THE MAN WHO PROVED IT'S POSSIBLE

There was a gentleman who drummed up the attention of the national media back in 2015 and thereafter. His name was Ronald Read, and he was from Brattleboro, Vermont. Mr. Read hadn't previously attracted any newsworthy attention. In fact, he had lived a quiet life under the radar as a janitor at JCPenney. He went to work, ate his muffin and sipped his coffee at the memorial hospital cafeteria each morning, and quietly went about his business.

He worked for years, eventually retired, and later passed away. It was at that time that something extraordinary was revealed. So what was it about him that made his legacy the topic of newspapers, websites, and widespread conversation? Read was about to single-handedly dispel the popular financial myth that we commonly buy into—that great wealth is not achievable by the everyday person.

Six million dollars bequeathed to the local library and hospital. That was Read's legacy. And with that, he would become one of the most unassuming philanthropists our nation has ever known. This would shock even his close family and friends, who believed him to be of modest means—a fitting assumption about someone living on a janitor's salary. But that $6 million wasn't the sum of Read's financial legacy. An additional $2 million in assets was distributed from his estate to his family, friends, and caregivers.

Read caught everyone off guard in a good way, impacting the people in his community and making headlines. His story continues to be shared to this day.

Read didn't have an outlandish income as a janitor. He didn't launch and sell a unicorn start-up in Silicon Valley. He didn't receive a weighty inheritance from his predecessors. Instead, he was able to do this because of his ongoing choice to consistently grow his money. He was normal, just like you and me. But what about Read can convince us to adopt the same squirreling-away technique he employed?

For one, he was clearly focused on his why. Now, I have to conjecture a bit here. Can you imagine him chuckling under his breath as he thought about how, in spite of all the books he had borrowed from the Brooks Memorial Library, they wouldn't be expecting a $1.2 million dollar gift in return? Can you just imagine the glee he felt every day as he went about amassing his fortune? Record-breaking glee. Perhaps his motive was to surprise and bless others. To leave lasting support for facilities that had not only benefited him, but would also continue to benefit the community. I can picture him imagining the look on the librarian's face as the check was opened, their eyes widening and jaw dropping. Read's were the largest gifts that either the library or hospital he gave to had ever received.

> *"Small everyday advancements make work light and progress certain."*

Read also understood the multiplying power of money and acted upon this consistently.

A curious young member of a group I coached once asked me out of the blue, "What brings success?" Now, that is a great question that could lead down any number of paths. Within the conversation that followed, we discussed that success is not a sudden occurrence for most of us. It's not inventing the next big thing. It's not the lifestyle a sudden, fortunate windfall brings. For most of us, success comes from doing the right thing every day, day in and day out.

Small everyday advancements make work light and progress certain. We look up and we're crossing a finish line because of all the steps we've taken prior. And that's what Read, our janitor, did. He received his paycheck and regularly put it in a place where it could grow, and it became what we feel is an impossible amount using possible means.

This should inspire us. We may not become multimillionaire philanthropists like Read did, but we can each optimize our finances to score high in our own financial lives. Read's story dispels the myth that financial wellness is not possible for the average person.

Not only did Read benefit his local library and hospital, he also left a message for us all. He was the David who vanquished the Goliath in all of our lives. He showed that the humble can conquer the great, that we too can slay our own giants. What our culture thinks is extraordinary can be a little more ordinary. Read's $8 million legacy is a Goliath of its own. But maybe it makes increasing our savings more fathomable for us. We can allow his accomplishment to have a gravitational pull on our finances. In fact, the amount of money an average American has at retirement age is only a small fraction of what Read saved up—about 1/30th the size, to give some context.

"It is tranquil people that accomplish much." That's a quote attributed to Henry David Thoreau. And how fitting that it appeared along with Read's photo in his high school yearbook from 1940. And pause and think about how the $8 million in wealth he gave away was his leftovers after he had already retired for 17 years.

Taking inspiration from Ronald Read's story, how do we shed our old selves and start anew? How do we make a sudden change from financial passivity to financial flourishing? We look for a turning point. As you read these pages, let them be that turning point for you. Take financial freedom by the reins. If not now, then when?

THE IMPORTANCE OF A TURNING POINT

Frustrated with being called shy during my grade school years, I desperately wanted to break free from those bonds of self-consciousness. I yearned to become confident and able to speak up. But how was I going to redefine myself?

The perfect turning point presented itself.

In high school, speech was a required class. During the first few days, I noticed I barely knew anyone in the room, and that was something I could take advantage of. While my classmates in other classes had a preconceived notion of me, no one in speech class knew me as the introvert I was. I had a chance to reinvent myself, and no one would be the wiser. What if I was suddenly outgoing while giving my first speech? No transition. No slow ramp-up. No semester-long change. Just right away, outgoing during the first speech.

And then I remembered my father's unique approach to solving problems he had modeled for me. It was time to think differently. After some crucial coaching from a friend who had previously taken the class, I was off with a plan that would break the mold for my introductory speech. Instead of standing up and presenting from the front of the class, I walked up and down each row visiting individual students, focusing on them one by one and delivering statements to them directly for all to hear.

As the speech got off the ground, I noticed anticipation built up for each unique encounter. The engagement kept rising, and the class was poised to react or even erupt in laughter as the momentum continued. That particular method of delivery proved to hold remarkable value, drawing in the whole class the whole time. It wasn't about being an expert orator. And with finances, it's not about being an expert either. In each case, it can be about a simple approach.

That initial talk in speech class would go down in history with my instructor, Mr. Eyman. It set me on a sudden course to a series of high-impact speeches as a newly "extroverted" speech deliverer. Those talks earned me the title of Speech King from my classmates. Was this new me the real me? By the time the year ended, Mr. Eyman had roped me in to perform in the talent show and had also awarded me the high school's first lettering in the category of Speech.

Years later, I'd find myself with a microphone in front of crowds of people for other unrelated reasons, sharing about my life—sometimes even in stadiums. The self-redefining moment I experienced in high school was no slow transition. This was a relatively major life change for a teenager that led to bigger outcomes and experiences. The label of introvert I had worn my whole life was shed all because I made use of a turning point during speech class. I was no longer experiencing impostor syndrome. This new me became the real me.

What could we trigger if we followed this sort of instant change in other categories of life? What I learned was we just need to get started. So, let's set off on our journey to seek a solution with money. We're all in. Let's shed the competing myths that this is not for us or we're not capable or deserving of improved financial well-being. We might just set ourselves up for a totally different outcome by leaning in.

Starting, no matter how small the start, is the important thing. You don't need to be sinless before you step in a church, you don't need to be clean before you take a shower, and you don't need to wield expert-level financial prowess on your journey to saving. Let's just get started on seeking a solution with money. You're not an impostor. This is possible.

MAKING THE TIME TO CHANGE

Starting on our path toward financial freedom may be our favorite thing to procrastinate on, but it takes relatively little time to do, considering the big picture. Take into consideration that people in the U.S. on average live 76 years. The following is an astounding statistic, but, when the hours are added up consecutively, about nine years of our lives are spent watching television around the clock. That's an astronomical 78,000 hours of television! We might expend about five years nonstop on social media platforms, or the equivalent of over 43,000 hours. And we allocate over 10 years' worth of time around the clock to working a job via about 90,000 hours in a lifetime.

By comparison, reading a nonfiction book such as this one may take less than four hours. You're spending some of those hours right now. Maybe you borrowed from some of those 78,000 hours of television to do it. But as we dedicate a relatively small amount of time to learning finances, the amazing thing about hearing just the right thing is that it may have redirecting power—the power to change our path in a good way, like a rudder can redirect a massive ship. Spending a week with financial education and a day making some changes can result in a massive difference in the end. The income we earn over those 90,000 hours of work mentioned previously is available to be redirected toward a greater impact. I'd say that's time well spent.

"A consistent activity, plus time, equals astronomical results."

If we sat on a couch in Seattle and didn't move, we'd still be on that couch 120 days later. But if we spent those same 120 days walking, we would end up traveling from Seattle to New York in that time. If the world were walkable along the equator, we could do a complete lap in three and a half years. If we walked for 40 years, we could walk around the world more than 11 times. A consistent activity, plus time, equals astronomical results.

In the same way, if we don't save, we'll have nothing later. But if we set aside money regularly, we might surprise ourselves with the results. Action versus inaction is one of the most important decisions you can make in life. You are determining long-term outcomes each time you adopt and carry out a habit.

OUR COMMON ENEMY

We've put in some effort, preparing ourselves to think differently. We've learned from my father's baseball strategies that simplifying can lead to success. William Kamkwamba's windmill story laid out the steps to having an epiphany. Ronald Read proved to us that financial wellness is possible for the everyday person. My speech class served as a reminder that we can start fresh at any time. And we found that it only takes a relatively short amount of time to shift our lives toward a healthier financial future. Now we'll move on from Seeking a Solution, which is the first step of experiencing an epiphany, to the second step, The Struggle.

Do we tell ourselves we make good money but ask where it all goes? Do we find ourselves burdened by all the financial information out there, lacking the initiative to take decisive action? Have we realized we need to increase our savings and improve our investing habits but have been unable to get ourselves to take action yet?

In order to overcome these and other mental blocks, we first must plainly identify them. There are six offenders that tend to distract us from making better financial decisions. Let's call these all-too-common menaces out from the shadows. In the next chapter, we'll expose them, name them, and study them in order to overcome them.

Chapter Review:
You're Not an Impostor—This Is possible

- **The Man Who Proved It's Possible:** The story of Ronald Read, the janitor who invested, helps show that we can choose to invest, multiply money, and do good with the results, regardless of our income.
- **The Importance of a Turning Point:** We've opted in to learning about finances by reading this book. Now is the time to make a change to reset our financial path. Seize this opportunity and don't delay.
- **Making the Time to Change:** It takes a relatively short amount of time to redirect our financial future for a massive impact. The sooner we start, the more years we have to leverage.
- **Our Common Enemy:** Before we play offense, we must play defense with our finances by seeing who we are up against.

Action Item:

You're Not an Impostor—This Is Possible

Making Your First Investment: First steps are the hardest. That's why I'm providing you with a guide on how to make your first investment. It'll get you started. And once you're going, the momentum will build. Download the *Financial Epiphany* Money Moves guide to get familiar with moves you can make with your money and access a curation of other invaluable insights: financialepiphany.com/moneymoves.

STEP 2

The Struggle

Each of us is held back by almost exactly the same six issues.

Chapters:

CHAPTER 3

What's Blocking Us from Having an Epiphany?

The Struggle step of experiencing an epiphany can feel counterproductive or even futile. Why would we opt in to walking ourselves down a path of potential mental roadblocks and exasperation? However, this phase creates the energy needed for us to travel forward with great force, providing the momentum our mind needs to break through our mental and behavioral barriers. The Struggle step is actually a blessing because it trains our eyes to notice and value remarkable solutions—solutions we might otherwise overlook and neglect. If we don't experience trials, we don't build up the tension that eventually releases a meaningful aha moment.

Napoleon is quoted as stating, "A genius is the man who can do the average thing when everyone else around him is losing his mind." In our case, the cool-headed genius chooses to avoid temptation and the opportunities for negligence listed in this chapter. These barriers are like quicksand for the mind, submerging our thoughts and holding them captive. So, let's slow down, pause, and use our discernment. Those who thoroughly understand money do things the average population does not. We may not self-identify as geniuses, but we can certainly emulate what geniuses do.

The following six financial mental blocks explain both mental and behavioral hurdles that can block us from experiencing a realization with our money, and each of them has its very own mischievous twist. These are the financial concerns that can keep us up at night or hide in the shadows, stealing from our financial future. Let's study them so we can break their grasp or avoid them entirely.

MENTAL BLOCK #1: DEBT IS NOT OUR FRIEND

The first and most obvious of the six financial mental blocks is our attitude toward debt. This is the elephant in the room. We overspend, using up all our resources and creating stress and anxiety as a result. There's nothing left. We're essentially opting to shift money from our accounts to line someone else's pockets. It's very generous of us to do that over a lifetime. Going into debt is paying someone more than what something is worth in order to have it right away. The fact that we live in a consumer-driven, social media-sharing culture is a good portion of the fuel that feeds this fire. According to reporting via CNBC, over 60% of adults in the United States are said to be living paycheck to paycheck.

We walk this default path of overspending because it's the one we're presented with, the one most tread on by the crowd, a tempting valley to pass through. Do you hear the captivating melodies of the Greek mythological sirens luring you down it?

In psychologist Solomon Asch's investigation on conformity, a group of actors were trained to answer a question incorrectly. They were asked to match the length of one line to that of another line. Unknowing participants embedded in the group often conformed to that (incorrect) overall group opinion and suppressed their individual decision-making, even if the right answer was painfully obvious. It's hard to deviate, even if we're right in doing so. We are most comfortable being in the herd, even if the herd is going about something incorrectly. Reverend H. K. Williams points out, "If you fail to prepare you are preparing to fail." We must choose our financial steps with intentionality.

So how do we keep ourselves from taking steps down this popular path littered with continuous snares and traps? There's a crossroads that exists. Let's recognize where the path splits so we can reveal these hidden hazards for what they are and select the alternate route.

Now let's get familiar with how the most familiar debts are introduced into our lives: the Five Cs of Financial Debt.

The Five Cs of Financial Debt: Card

Unless we choose a path of financial wellness, our path to financial conformity starts when we receive credit card offers in the mail when we turn 18 years old. The Federal Reserve reports that 82% of adults carry at least one credit card. According to *Forbes*, about 13% of the U.S. population carries five or more cards. It's been said that carrying this plastic empowers us, giving us the ability to acquire shiny new things we may not have the ability to obtain otherwise. Most of us don't realize this empowerment comes with optional shackles that aren't immediately apparent.

Over half of us who have credit cards carry debt on them. This is the group the lending industry refers to as *revolvers*, those of us that allow balances to roll over, kicking into gear those double-digit interest rates—an unfavorable 20% or more in some cases. This habit means we're spending more than we can pay off. And again, more than half of us fall into this group. The average amount that gets carried over month to month is over $6,000, and around 90% of card companies' profits come from the habits of revolvers. By comparison, *transactors,* who pay off their cards each month, only comprise about 10% of the profits for card companies, generating profit primarily through merchant transaction fees.

Do ads, commercials, and marketing materials heavily influence our financial behavior? Marketers wouldn't pour billions of dollars into the marketing industry if it didn't work. In the United States, we spend over $400 billion annually on advertising—more than double what China, the runner-up, spends. The per capita spending on advertising per American is over $1,000 per year and is steadily increasing. The authors of *Your Money or Your Life*, Vicki Robin and Joe Dominguez, ask, "What kind of society turns its young people into a profit center for the debt industry?" Consumerism makes our nation go 'round. Feeling patriotic? If spending is a measure of our allegiance, then we have the most patriotic population ever.

The Five Cs of Financial Debt: College

The next C that comes knocking on our door is college—or rather, college debt. Sixty percent of Americans who attend higher education take out loans to attend learning institutes that are more expensive than they have the money for. Some professions require more extensive schooling, but for many of us, there are more affordable options.

The average amount of college debt is over $30,000. How are students supposed to understand the weight of $30,000 or $60,000 or $100,000+ in tuition debt when they've never dealt with those numbers before? We're asking teenagers to make decisions with whopping big price tags! We've been told that teen brains are still developing during that time, yet they're being asked to sign on the dotted line on a life-altering matter. They are asked to trust the academic system to ensure that everything will get sorted out.

One of the reasons college debt is such a significant risk to our financial potential is that it introduces a 10-year on-average debt of about $400 per month. Millions of us default on these loans each year, meaning we're failing to pay them back. When we take out student loans, we are buying something we can't afford, and the world is letting us. Collectively, we are normalizing the invitation of student loans into our lives—44 million Americans are burdened by them at any given time.

The Five Cs of Financial Debt: Car

Let's look at another likely step in our financial journey: car. Their commercials are cut quickly, like music videos—they're seductive. Cars appeal to our desire for status. There's hardly anything our culture depends on more to say, "If I own this, people will think I'm successful." Cars are the all-American status symbol. The ads we see don't give attention to the total cost of the vehicle but redirect our gaze toward the monthly payment. But how many months of payments will be required of us? And what amount of interest will be paid over the life of the loan?

Many types of advertising serve as lures, bobbing for our attention and diverting us from the hidden hooks behind. But if our true, authentic financial situations were exposed for all to see, many of us would be wearing potato sacks as we posed next to our sleek, sophisticated automobiles with hefty payment plans.

The Five Cs of Financial Debt: Cake

Whether it's joining others on vacations we can't afford, lavishly sharing restaurant meals with friends, or even overspending on our wedding cakes, we love shelling out for celebrations and experiences. There's pressure to spend without regard when peer pressure is on. Many of us allocate more time toward planning vacations than we put toward planning our financial well-being.

For weddings in particular, there may be 50, 100, or 150-plus attendees, all enjoying the party we've assembled. Society looks at our weddings as a reflection on us. That's a lot of expectation. What kind of venue, dress, tux, catering, flowers, or wedding favors did we select? Did we think of—and pay handsomely for—every little detail?

According to Bill Fay of Debt.org, the average wedding stacks up to $30,000 in bills, of which $10,000 is borrowed. It's more than a little ironic that financial woes are a leading cause of divorce. So don't start off walking down the aisle on the wrong foot by introducing money problems for you and your spouse to stew over once the wedding bells have stopped. Give yourselves a real wedding gift and stay out of debt from the get-go.

Travel, celebrations, and other experiences all call out to us and our wallets. Together, these costs of life can serve as emotional experiences that open the door for debt to easily waltz on in.

The Five Cs of Financial Debt: Condo

We all need a place to live, and many of us will choose to own the four walls and roof that give us shelter, whether those walls make up a condo, house, or apartment. About two-thirds will purchase, while one-third of us will rent. But with what will likely be the single largest purchase or ongoing cost of our lives, how do we know how much to spend? Experts recommend that we spend no more than 25% to 30% of our take-home pay per month on housing. However, many of us are tempted to buy or rent more house than we should, whether to serve our own comforts or to impress others. The lesson here is to avoid becoming "house poor" by having too large a proportion of our paychecks disappear to pay for our living quarters each month.

The Five Cs of Financial Debt

So, do you get the villain of our story? Do you get our debt problem? Each debt we incur can move us farther behind our own financial starting line. Each debt takes us a few steps backward. Think of dealing with personal finance like running a race. Who would intentionally don a heavy burden before the starting gun fires? But that's what we do. See in the following graph for what these five typical debts of life look like charted out, using approximate average values: maintaining $6,000 of credit card debt, borrowing $10,000 to fund our wedding or other experiences, signing up for $23,000 in loans per car owned, paying back $38,000 for college, and having $330,000 in mortgage payments.

A Look at the Five Cs of Financial Debt

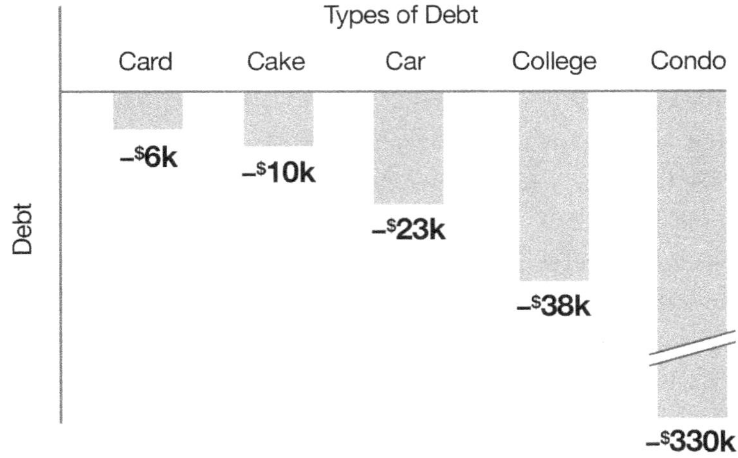

And some of those are not one-time debts. Credit cards tend to stick around as an ongoing debt, each American purchases about eight cars over their lifetime, and we may purchase two or three homes throughout our lives. So many of these debts, and the choice to repeat bad habits, can occur over and over again across a lifetime. If we were on the lookout for money to save and multiply, we've found it. This is what's holding us back. There's no required price tag on each of these items. There are choices. We can choose to save up ahead of time for the expense, we can choose to work the cost off as we go, or we can choose a more affordable route.

"Do we snuggle with our struggle?"

Spending less than we make has never been more important than it is now as the world is getting more expensive to live in. When more freedom and impact are written into our story, we erase them off the page willingly by taking for today. We may even protect, defend, and justify our debt—"But it was on sale." "But we got points." "But I just had to have it." We hide our debt from view, denying that it's a hindrance, giving it permission to hang around as long as it pleases. Do we snuggle with our struggle? We might even assign it a friendlier name like *financing* or *payment plan*.

Many admit, "If I knew what I know now before I took on debt, I would have done things differently." We tend to have that shared hindsight regarding debt. In fact, I like debt about as much as I like having a tortilla chip stab me in the roof of the mouth. But here's the thing. We are in front of the next pitfalls coming, and we can avoid them. Relieving ourselves of debt is how we evade or overcome the first and by far biggest of the six financial mental blocks. We must shift our minds away from spending.

Now on to identifying our second financial mental block that stands in the way of our journey to an epiphany.

MENTAL BLOCK #2: CRISIS, CRISIS, CRISIS

Americans are notorious for overspending. We're also notorious for living paycheck to paycheck. Currently, many Americans spend as much as we make every two weeks, and chances are low that we would be able to handle a $400 financial emergency without having to borrow money.

Why did we fall into a housing crisis? Why is there an impending retirement crisis? Why are we in a student loan crisis? *Crisis, crisis, crisis.* Shouldn't crises be rare? We're juggling crises. If crises are normal, we accept them into our lives. We go with the flow. We normalize the risk. As a nation, we are tens of trillions of dollars in debt. That breaks down to tens of thousands of dollars per head…even counting the babies! We're riding a wave of debt. But as riding waves tends to go, we're more likely to wipe out than experience a smooth ride.

Dangling on the edge of a cliff carefree is not normal behavior. However, surprisingly, we've become very comfortable with this everyday risk with our finances to the point that it almost seems like no risk at all. Little by little, we've sauntered to the edge of the ridge together and taken a seat right there, keeping each other company. Since we're all there together, the inherent danger doesn't seem dangerous at all—in fact, everyone's doing it. But as we know, a sudden market disruption, recession, pandemic, or job loss can cause the edge of that cliff to crumble at a moment's notice.

MENTAL BLOCK #3: FEAR, TRUST, AND RISK

Money has traditionally been thought of as a dry, uninteresting, intimidating thing. It's a completely miserable topic for the majority of us, associated with fear, regret, and even shame—especially when we're talking about our own personal dealings with it. Many of us are afraid we've been mishandling money, and we put off revealing our checkered past with it. We close our eyes, hoping our missteps will go away. We may not know what to do, even if we do feel ready to become educated on it. Maybe we've made mistakes. Maybe we've faced money failures in the past. That feeling is common. We can overcome it as we set our gaze forward to do better in the future.

It's easy to focus on the fact that the market (stocks, bonds, and other financial assets) as a whole sometimes goes down in value, regardless of the investment vehicle we choose to put money into. Our initial step into trusting in the market can be hard. But it can feel much better once we've taken action and seen results. Many common types of assets are not fully protected from temporarily taking a dip. We might be so averse to that possibility we'd be willing to look past the positive side—that the market has continually gained value in the long run, despite any forfeits.

Warren Buffett, famed investor and cofounder of Berkshire Hathaway, once said, "Our unwavering conclusion: Never bet against America." This statement points to his long-standing belief in the fortitude and resourcefulness of the American economy. There's trust he holds in the self-propelling nature of American business. Life always has some element of risk we'll need to accept. And in life, we'll live through some economic recessions. We'll all get through them together. And just as a rising tide lifts all boats, a lowering tide tends to include most everyone as well. But we all ride these tides together.

It's quite normal to fantasize about making fast money, whether through speculative investments, gambling, listening to a friend's latest risky single stock tip, or pouring money into the lottery. We may desire to hit a savings goal too aggressively or hope to make up for what we feel is lost time. But these are all distractions that can act like a black hole, sucking up all our money and never giving it back.

Let's take the lottery, for example. It's common to enjoy the mental pastime of contemplating winning the lottery, even if we're among those who don't buy tickets! But the statistics don't lie—more than 60% of us actually do play a form of the lottery. And we hand over, on average, $86 per month to it. That's over $1,000 a year per person. And we still only have about a one in 7 million chance of winning a state lottery, or a one in 300 million chance of winning the Mega Millions or Powerball jackpot. Even for smaller winnings, the return on investment is typically $0 or even negative. We must take our minds off risky distractions and focus on the clear and steady win. That's an actual lifestyle we're talking about here—no longer a lottery dream.

MENTAL BLOCK #4: ANALYSIS PARALYSIS

What causes us to pause when it comes to changing our financial behavior? There's a litany of obstacles that halt us in our tracks. We tend to find ourselves thwarted by financial information overload. So many things to know and so many competing voices. Many of us freeze in place, unable to move or adjust our finances. We experience analysis paralysis. We become stunned, falling into a state of inaction.

We are in desperate need of a refreshing path to walk our money down. But no one in our lives is officially assigned to teach us about money, we aren't shown who to trust regarding money matters, and we're told not to talk about it. I'd say that's a very buttoned-up and well-packaged problem delivered right to our doorsteps. When I was younger, my mother used to say that talking about money was like talking about our underwear. It was a private topic!

As we enter adult life, just because we've grown up doesn't mean we've all been suddenly rewired to filter the varied financial messages of the world. Maybe you don't connect with the way finances have been explained to you. But this is what the world seems to expect of us: to homogenize expectations when it comes to money. The world insists we all equally enjoy thumbing through 401(k) documentation, fine print, and financial prospectuses as we cozy up to a fire. It assumes we're old enough to figure financial matters out on our own. But the world couldn't be more wrong. More of us need help than ever before!

MENTAL BLOCK #5: KEEPING UP WITH THE JONESES

In 1913, Arthur R. "Pop" Momand developed a comic strip that found widespread popularity, becoming a cultural phenomenon across the United States. The theme expressed in the cartoon would find its way into our modern-day financial lives. Aloysius, the central character, was similar in appearance to the Monopoly man—a short, stocky fellow with a handlebar mustache, top hat, and monocle. He strained with constant effort as he attempted to match the lavish lifestyle of his neighbors, the Joneses. However, he continually failed to reach that elusive goal, unable to emulate his neighbors' affluence. The title of the strip, *Keeping Up with the Joneses*, would continue past the life of the actual comic, enduring as its own frequently stated idiom.

Syndicated in over 100 newspapers across the country, the printed piece provided humor for over 25 years. There was that much comedy to pull from the simple topic of chasing after our neighbors' wealth. But today, "keeping up with the Joneses" is not just remembered as a weekly comic strip and source for laughs—it has very real influence on our purchasing behaviors.

How much do we care about what people think of us? Most of us put a lot of stock in it, whether we know it or not. It's prudent to be able to recognize how much our circles and communities are influencing us. Have friends who are vacationing well, dining out, and living the high life? There's no need to compare ourselves to them—we should stay focused on the optimization of our own finances.

Spending money to impress people is the fastest way to lose that money. We see each other's possessions, but we can't see if there's actually anything left sitting in each other's bank accounts. If we spend money on things, we end up with the things but no money. Having things makes us *feel* rich, but keeping money is *being* rich. This preoccupation with keeping up our image serves as a distraction from having an epiphany with our money.

Now on to the sixth and final mental block.

MENTAL BLOCK #6: LIFESTYLE INFLATION

As we make more money in life, we end up spending more. It's like we're in our own financial arms race, a cold war with ourselves. This behavior is called lifestyle inflation. We can't ever seem to make enough to save. We can't seem to catch up. We're chasing our own tails.

According to the online job search site Zippia, many of us will earn around $2 million over our working lives, but few of us will seek education or best practices on how to steward that monumental amount of funds. Can you imagine if $2 million suddenly dropped in your lap? Many of us would immediately seek out an emergency meeting with a financial advisor for direction. But because we are paid those funds incrementally over a working life and receive raise by raise annually, we pay less heed. A lifetime is a long time to do something well—or not so well. For the average person, a lifetime consists of 76 years, or over 27,740 days. So where are we headed on our 27,740-day financial journey? Are we being intentional in our steps?

Certainly, expenses mount in life as we age: raising a child, paying more bills, covering a mortgage, taking care of aging parents. But one factor in action here is the hedonic treadmill. The concept explains how, even after acquiring more stuff, we don't feel any different. This is the resetting of our hedonic set point, a constantly roving internal sensor that tells us that no matter how much effort we put into becoming happier, we'll float around our baseline. So, is there a need to constantly make more purchases? To make bigger purchases? Probably not. Let's direct ourselves away from this mental block.

THE PATH OF SNARES AND TRAPS

The formula for experiencing an epiphany commonly includes The Struggle, the step we've just walked through. It's a path ridden with mental snares and traps that occupy our minds away from being constructive with our funds. We have ourselves to thank for this, as much of our own financial struggle may be due to our participation in some of the hindering thinking and behaviors we've just discussed. But identifying and naming those thoughts and behaviors gives us power over them. The six financial mental blocks we just discussed are no longer menaces that can slip into our party without being on the guest list. We can stare these habits in the eye and tell them they're not welcome.

Some of this may have stung a little to hear, but it's best to pull the sliver from our foot before we step into the next leg of our journey. We've done our due diligence to this point and endured the critique. Congratulations—it's not usually a comfortable experience. And with that, we've now waded through the second step of introducing a financial epiphany into our lives, The Struggle. We are now primed for the third step, Coming to a Realization.

Chapter Review:

What's Blocking Us from Having an Epiphany?

- **Mental Block #1: Debt Is Not Our Friend:** Americans tend to take out debt via the five Cs of financial debt: card, college, car, cake, and condo.
- **Mental Block #2: Crisis, Crisis, Crisis:** The student loan crisis, housing crisis, and retirement crisis all point to one thing: we've normalized crises!
- **Mental Block #3: Fear, Trust, and Risk:** It's common for our relationship and history with money to feel like a dysfunctional one. If that's how you feel, you're not alone!
- **Mental Block #4: Analysis Paralysis:** With so much to know about money and so many choices to be made about our financial situation, we can feel overwhelmed and intimidated with so many choices. This can freeze us from acting.
- **Mental Block #5: Keeping Up with the Joneses:** Our spending may in part be fueled by our desire for status.
- **Mental Block #6: Lifestyle Inflation:** The more money we make over a lifetime, the more our spending tends to grow. Many of us will earn $2 million over a lifetime. How are we preparing to handle that sum?
- **The Path of Snares and Traps:** If we don't choose a path for ourselves, the world is happy to walk us down one with financial temptations aplenty. We must avoid these traps to free up our money for the multiplying it is capable of.

Action Items:

What's Blocking Us from Having an Epiphany?

- **The Five Cs of Financial Debt:** List how much debt you owe in each category: card, college, car, cake, and condo. Separate out individual debts, listing any other debts outside of these categories as well.
- **The Debt Snowball:** From the list of debts above, plan on attacking the smallest debt by paying it off early. Continue on to the remaining debts from smallest to largest. More freedom awaits as you juggle fewer separate debts over time and psychologically experience momentum.
- **Deleting Debt:** Download the *Financial Epiphany* Money Moves guide and start making moves to climb out of debt—and, more importantly, avoid future debt from here on out. Find it at financialepiphany.com/moneymoves.

STEP 3

Coming to a Realization

Unleash your money-multiplying superpower.

Chapters:

CHAPTER 4

First Comes the Framework

Robbie Gonzalez, writer for *WIRED*, was taught to solve a Rubik's cube by Tyson Mao of the World Cube Association. After several days, Gonzalez reduced his solve time from 45 minutes to an average of under a minute. In a video for *WIRED*, Gonzalez identified the steps he now takes to solve a Rubik's Cube, sharing his process publicly in about as friendly and inviting a manner as can be.

My son challenged me to learn the cube, so I committed to solving it alongside him. But could someone like me acquire this skill? I felt like an impostor. What was at stake? My pride collapsing in front of my son if he was able to learn it and I could not? Letting my son down if he struggled with the process and I was not able to serve as a guiding light, if I was in over my head?

With six colored sides and 54 individual outer surfaces, a Rubik's Cube has over 43 quintillion possible configurations. That's a couple more commas and sets of zeros over and beyond a trillion. When my son and I took on this challenge, this proliferous plaything—of which several varieties have been sitting in my house for years—finally had nowhere to hide. We were going to place that cube squarely on the dining room table in plain sight each night, and we were going to overcome that mentally elusive toy.

But here is the key. There was a particular framework we used for learning the cube. Of the several approaches and techniques available for solving the three-dimensional puzzle, we sought out and settled on Gonzalez's method. According to that method, the bottom layer must be solved first. Then you move on to the middle layer. Finally, you complete the top layer. That's the order of attack. I hadn't been aware of it before, but that general approach takes the multicolored mystery and applies a framework to it. What I had previously observed to be a shifting box of infinite approaches now had one approach: bottom, middle, then top.

Without any direction, it would have been punishing to learn the toy. We didn't have to spend a month, day in and day out, like the toy's inventor, Ernő Rubik, to painstakingly figure out the necessary algorithms on our own. We simply followed someone who had laid out only the steps we needed to know using an easy-to-grasp method. Now, there are special movements to practice, patterns to recognize, and even algorithms to internalize with the cube, but those are all packed within those three larger steps—what I refer to as a simple framework.

SIMPLE FRAMEWORKS SET THE LEARNER UP FOR SUCCESS

Just like the simple framework set up for learning the Rubik's Cube, we'll start out with a simple framework for learning about multiplying money. With a solid, static foundation in place, we'll simplify the process rather than complicate our learning with constantly roving variables. There are a host of distractions—the many intimidating and conflicting messages the world of finance has to offer—that would like to blow this house down.

The best way to learn is simply and within a protected environment. Once we get comfortable with *simple*, we can choose to apply our learning to other scenarios. There's a set of three principles we'll start with to build upon. I call this the Simple Framework. This framework will serve as a consistent foundation underlying the teachings to follow. We'll take our initial glance here and be sure to restate these three principles from time to time to remind ourselves as we move forward.

OUR SIMPLE FRAMEWORK

Principle #1: Starting Work at Age 22

Many young adults start careers at age 22. Often this follows years of college. For simplicity, rather than elaborating on each and every potential age for starting a career, we'll select the age 22 to use in our framework as we move forward.

Principle #2: 40 Years of Work

People generally work about a 40-year career before they retire. Keeping our first principle in mind, our Simple Framework focuses on ages 22 to 62. Money can be further multiplied beyond that, but this principle is here to keep us focused on understanding the multiplying power we have during the span of the typical 40-year career.

Principle #3: Earning a 7.2% Rate of Return

Let's talk about rate of return. That's the money that money earns. A savings account earns a rate of return. Stocks earn a rate of return. Bonds earn a rate of return. Various money instruments such as these invite us to place money into them, and the reward is a profit. With risk comes reward, and that can hold true here. The safety and security of a savings account at a bank may bring a low rate of return, while stocks, with their more volatile ups and downs, have been known to bring a relatively higher rate of return over time. Popular retirement accounts like the 401(k) or individual retirement account (IRA) may include investment assets like index funds or mutual funds. These funds may contain a bundle of stocks and bonds. Not very familiar with placing money into any of these stated vehicles yet? No problem—we'll discuss that later.

Part of the reason for this book is to empower you to invest money in order to grow it, even if you haven't done so yet. The market will go up and down, and your personal tolerance for risk and choice of asset can lead to varied results, but to keep things simple, 7.2%[1] is a great number to learn by. You'll see why. This book follows a simple stream of thought, but the appendix contains several other scenarios using different rates of return if you're interested. Complexity is introduced once we try to solve for every scenario, so once again, we'll teach here with 7.2% in mind.

For the purposes of simplicity and to establish a baseline, we'll

---

1 For more information on a 7.2% annualized rate of return, see the rule of 72 on page 171. Reinvested dividends and company-matching retirement plans help even more with the attainment of such a return on your initial personal investment.

also leave out the impacts that company contributions,[2] taxes, inflation, and fees can have on investments. They can certainly be present, but they lay outside the protected learning environment that our Simple Framework provides. Remember how my father coached us six-year-old baseball players? He started out simple, but we didn't stay playing that way for long. As we won games from the get-go by employing simple tactics, we gradually learned the more complex rules of baseball and graduated to playing in a more sophisticated manner. We'll take the same approach with our finances, allowing ourselves to first be empowered to understand and act and then have the option to invite in sophistication once we're ready.

All right, that's it. We've gone over the three principles of our Simple Framework:

Principle #1: Starting Work at Age 22

Principle #2: 40 Years of Work

Principle #3: Earning a 7.2% Rate of Return

We'll learn with these principles in mind, and if your path is different, you'll be able to adjust for your scenario. And with that, we're equipped to proceed to cover the three financial epiphanies. Ready?

---

2 Employers may choose to offer company matching or company contributions to employee retirement plans, thus boosting the invested amount.

CHAPTER 5

Financial Epiphany #1: Doubling Years

It's time now to start down the rabbit hole. Thinking differently with finances is done best while maintaining proper focus. So, let's guard our time, fixate our minds, and dive in with the first of the three financial epiphanies—doubling years.

THE MOST FAMOUS EPIPHANIES

Perhaps the most well-known epiphany in history occurred with Sir Isaac Newton, the English mathematician who is said to have witnessed a falling apple. *Why should that apple always descend perpendicularly to the ground?* he thought to himself. And this same phenomenon that pulled the apple to the ground, why would that same force not reach as high as the moon and influence its orbit?

Newton began making a connection in his mind that localized occurrences, such as a falling apple, and a distant and mysterious occurrence, like the orbiting moon, could be pointing to the very same principle of the galaxy: gravity. And he was right.

Likewise, we'll now build associations in our minds to aid and bolster our understanding of money.

Now on to historical story number two.

According to legend, Archimedes, the Greek mathematician, experienced a sudden insight as he stepped into his bathtub. As he settled his body in the water, he noticed the level of the water rise, even spilling out. That experience jolted his mind, and he realized when an object is placed into water, the weight of water it displaces helps calculate the buoyancy of that object. Because he had struggled to understand this principle, the seemingly unrelated activity of taking a bath led him to experience an epiphany. His mind was primed and ready to have each and every task in his life stimulate his mind in relation to the topic of buoyancy—even such a seemingly mundane task as an evening bath.

Upon realizing what he had stumbled upon, Archimedes allegedly became so excited that he left his bath behind, running unclothed through the city streets, exclaiming, "Eureka! Eureka!" meaning, "I have found it! I have found it!" Whether that part of the story is myth or fact, it illustrates how exhilarating discovery can be.

Sir Isaac Newton is said to have experienced an epiphany when he witnessed a falling apple, Archimedes was prompted by running a bath, and William Kamkwamba, our young inventor from our first chapter who built a windmill, was motivated by a bicycle. The extraordinary thing here is that neither an apple, a bathtub, or a bicycle come across as extraordinary items on their own. They are all basic, everyday, non-eureka-type things. Yet each was a key puzzle piece that inspired an incredible realization.

THE MARSHMALLOW TEST

The marshmallow test, a defining moment in the exploration of human behavior, was a study conducted in 1972 at Stanford University by psychologist Walter Mischel. His experiment sought to study immediate versus delayed gratification. Self-control and patience, or lack thereof, were on display.

The premise of the experiment was simple: a single marshmallow was placed before a young child who was given the option to either eat it or wait. If the child consumed the marshmallow, that was all he got. Experiment over. At that point, he may have been considered a subject of his own immediate gratification. Or—rewind!—he could conversely choose to wait a select number of minutes, and if he exerted the necessary self-control to leave the white, spongy treat untouched, he was rewarded with a second marshmallow.

Children who resisted enticement practiced delayed gratification. Delayed gratification, the study found, was correlated with later success in many measures of life, including achievement in schooling, relationships, resistance to substance abuse, and more. The results of the study have been contested since then, but for our case, we're focusing on just the following:

One marshmallow...wait. Then we get two.

Simple, right? Maybe too simple on the surface. Like a door leading down a passageway to hidden treasures, there's more here to be had. More to be revealed. And with that, here's where we have our chance to go beyond the initial experiment. If this principle holds true, why stop at two marshmallows? What if we choose to extrapolate on this scenario? Like a good movie or book that leaves you wanting more, in this case there's nothing stopping us from continuing the story ourselves. Is there a way to earn more marshmallows?

If a two-marshmallow child were to wait further, could she now double her results to receive four marshmallows total?

And what if she continued to wait more from there with her four marshmallows? To follow the pattern, she should be rewarded with eight marshmallows in all.

And if she exercised self-control yet again, shouldn't that result in an inventory of 16 marshmallows? Is there no limit to this? Well, at this point our young multiplying hero might as well pop some marshmallows in her mouth while the remaining treats continue to proliferate. Going back to the concept of delayed gratification, with her ability to wait for reward, this girl opened up the door to a life lesson on exponential growth and blooming opportunity.

OVERLAP WITH PERSONAL FINANCES

Does this marshmallow-doubling-over-time phenomenon exist outside the laboratory? Absolutely. This, in fact, totally and almost too conveniently overlaps with a real-life financial principle. Like a detective superimposing a fingerprint over another fingerprint, we've got a match here. Like one marshmallow turning into two, money behaves just the same—one dollar left for the right amount of time in the right place turns into two. And that right there is the foundation we'll build upon.

As we expound upon our framework for thinking about finances, we'll adopt the idea of money doubling. Money doubling is the foundation to our approach. By choosing to focus on money doubling, we're controlling the narrative. We're making money play on our terms, choosing one route to think along rather than being weighed down by all the options.

All right. To understand how the multiplying of a dollar occurs, let's get further into two factors regarding money: the right time and the right place.

THE RIGHT TIME

Given a normal rate of return—we're using 7.2% from our Simple Framework here—money that we invest doubles after 10 years. Ten years. We have to pause right here. We have to absolutely love this number. This is going to be the easiest calculation to make over our lifetimes, in all situations. Ten is, and always has been, one of the world's favorite numbers to multiply, divide, add, and subtract by. And it's most likely one you appreciate too, just like every kid in grade school does. An initial amount of money doubles every 10 years. Easy enough to remember.

Put in a dollar once, and after 10 years, even if you don't put in a dollar more, that initial amount can double to $2. Wait 10 more years, and it can double to $4. Wait again, and it turns to $8. Then it multiplies to $16...all without adding a dollar more than the initial amount. All you have to do is leave it alone to multiply. By starting with a single $1 input and simply waiting, you arrive at $16, an identical path to our doubling marshmallows.

Marshmallows and Money Doubling

		10 min	20 min	30 min	40 min
Marshmallows	**1**	**2**	**4**	**8**	**16**

		10 yrs	20 yrs	30 yrs	40 yrs
Money	**$1**	**$2**	**$4**	**$8**	**$16**

In the two grids above, you'll see how the overlap between how our marshmallows multiply and how money multiplies is uncanny. Something simple can now be used to explain something complex. Something inviting can now be used to explain something intimidating. These marshmallows can help bridge the gap for us in our quest to understand money.[3] We can immediately expound upon this. Instead of starting with $1, what would it look like if we started with $1,000? See the next grid.

Money Doubling

		10 yrs	20 yrs	30 yrs	40 yrs
Money	**$1,000**	**$2,000**	**$4,000**	**$8,000**	**$16,000**

[3] In Walter Mischel's marshmallow test, children were asked to wait 15 minutes before receiving a second marshmallow. We use 10 minutes in this chart to simplify the comparison being made.

THE RIGHT PLACE

So how does the first $1,000 turn to $2,000? We mention a normal rate of return. For more than one reason, 7.2% is a magical number when it comes to investing. It's the rate we use in our Simple Framework, introduced in the previous chapter. For one, it's a fairly normal rate of return per year. Invest $1,000 in an appropriate investment vehicle, and the following year, add on 7.2%, resulting in $1,072. The next year, that $1,072 adds on another 7.2%, calculated from that new, larger, cumulative total. Continue this for eight more years, and we reach the $2,000 mark mentioned above.

The market has appeared favorable toward 7.2%. Historically, the stock market has ranged between 7% and 10% over the long term.[4] That doesn't mean it always will, but for our rule of thumb, using this familiar rate of return leads to easy math. You'll see how.

Each of us must choose which investment vehicles to trust our money in, and also which risk/reward balance we're comfortable with. Many folks choose to invest through a retirement channel such as a 401(k) or IRA. Others may directly invest in index funds, mutual funds, exchange-traded funds (ETFs), and other such means to achieve such returns.[5] There is a host of options out there. But once again, 7.2% is the magic rate of return for our purposes. If we can maintain those sorts of earnings, calculating our finances remains surprisingly simple.

For some context, if we are able to achieve a higher rate of

---

4 Past performance is not a guarantee of future results. To see the effect of other annual rates of return, see the figure on page 174 of the appendix titled "Multiplying Money with Different Rates of Return" and the associated graphs.

5 More explanation of investment vehicles to come in chapter 8, "Let's Set Up Your Money Multiplying Machine."

return, such as 8%, that will double an initial investment in a shorter amount of time—after about nine years as opposed to 10. And a lower rate of return, such as 6%, will take longer to double money—about 12 years.

When investing, keep in mind that there are market fluctuations, potential employer matching on retirement accounts, reinvesting dividends, inflation, taxes, fees, and other possible variables to consider. As you might suspect from that long list, these are the things that can bring complexity back into the mix, so for now, we're focusing on our simplified tool that allows us to quickly understand and take action.

DOUBLING YEARS

Now let's crank up our understanding another notch within our Simple Framework. As you'll remember from principle #2, we're assuming most people work for an average of 40 years. That means with our framework here we, on average, have an opportunity to double money upon itself four times—four sets of 10 years. Here's how this one-time investment might play out for an average working person:

> 22 years old: We invest $10,000,[6] wait 10 years, and it doubles into $20,000 over that time.
>
> 32 years old: We don't touch the $20,000, wait 10 years, and it doubles into $40,000.
>
> 42 years old: We smile at the $40,000, wait 10 years, and it doubles into $80,000.

---

6 We are using $10,000 here for simple math. Some may be able to save this amount over one year of work, while others may find this goal attainable over a longer period of time.

52 years old: We laugh with disbelief at the $80,000, wait 10 years, and it doubles into $160,000.

62 years old: We retire and enjoy the fact that we just turned a one-time investment of $10,000 into $160,000.

That's a free $150,000 that we earned just by placing it in the market. It's all growth. We only put in an initial $10,000. Work smarter, not harder. Rather than putting in all the hours to earn a full $160,000, which might take the average person two or three years, we put to use only $10,000, which the average person makes in a couple months. *Wow—you mean we can do a couple months of work now and have the same impact dollarwise*[7] *as a few years of work later?* Yes. Are we feeling our leveraging power now?

These sets of years can be referred to as *doubling years*, the number of years it takes for our money to double. Here, that number of years is 10. And it's important to recognize how many sets of doubling years we have until we plan to stop working. In the case we're discussing, that's four sets, four opportunities to double our money upon itself in a working lifetime. Doubling years are based on a number of factors, such as our investment choices, how the market performs, and how conservative or aggressive we are in our investments. But, for the sake of keeping things simple, we'll continue to look at 10-year periods. One thing starts to become recognizable: things that are on track to double are set to increase exponentially.

---

7 Inflation will play a part in lessening the value of the dollar over time.

WHY ONLY LOOK AT A SINGLE INVESTMENT?

The marshmallow test places before each child a single marshmallow. There is beauty in that simplicity. And we're borrowing from that in our parallel storyline, where we only consider a single initial amount of money. By keeping our thinking simple, we hold off on considering all the complexities that block us from understanding money. We understand our input and the resulting output. One thousand dollars in becomes $16,000 later. And knowing both of those is the key to being empowered.

But don't people regularly contribute to their investment accounts via such routes as scheduled paycheck deductions? Yes—and it's highly recommended that we do invest regularly. However, the average person isn't often in the mood to compute the process of ongoing investment contributions in a meaningful way. I'd be the first to admit to that. Financial tools, calculators, and experts start to become necessary to lean on, and complexity sets in. We lose the glorious simplicity that comes from only thinking about a single investment, and we add a layer of distance between ourselves and comprehending the money we are investing. This is all about gaining personal ownership and understanding over our finances. We'll achieve this by keeping things simple within our learning ecosystem.

On to Financial Epiphany #2: The Power of 16.

Chapter Review:

Financial Epiphany #1: Doubling Years

- **The Most Famous Epiphanies:** Both Sir Isaac Newton's and Archimedes's stories show us that simple items, such as an apple or bathtub, can trigger immense realizations.
- **The Marshmallow Test:** This was a study that differentiated between instant and delayed gratification. The reward, a marshmallow, could be doubled in the experiment, simply by waiting.
- **Overlap with Personal Finances:** Just like marshmallows doubling in the marshmallow test, money-doubling is a simplified way to understand money.
- **The Right Time:** Money earning a 7.2% rate of return can double if invested for 10 years.
- **The Right Place:** Experts point out that a 7.2% rate of return has commonly been able to be achieved within a retirement account such as a 401(k) or IRA. Directly investing in index funds, mutual funds, and ETFs are other common methods of seeking that rate of return.
- **Doubling Years:** Over the average 40-year career, we have an opportunity to double money four times over—four sets of 10 years. An initial investment can double, double again, and again, and finally again.
- **Why Only Look at a Single Investment?:** Boiling things down to thinking in terms of a single investment is the key to simplifying and thus grasping understanding.

Action Items:

Financial Epiphany #1: Doubling Years

- **What Are You Invested In?:** Are you already investing? Log in to your associated online account or call your brokerage firm up and see how much is saved there. Check in on your account at least once a year to get familiar with seeing changes over time. Not investing yet? Then chapter 8, "Let's Set Up Your Money-Multiplying Machine," is for you.
- **What Rate of Return Do You Have?:** Log in to your online account and check what your annualized rate of return has been over the life of the account. This is a good number by which to gauge the rate at which your money is multiplying. Reference the chart "Multiplying Money with Different Rates of Return" on page 174 of the appendix to see the multiplying power your rate of return can bring to your money.

CHAPTER 6

Financial Epiphany #2: The Power of 16

One day, as I was sitting at the dining room table relaxing my mind, I percolated over why there are so many of us that are allergic to exponential growth. By that I mean the thought of saving a long, long time—say, throughout our typical 40-year work life. We have a resistance to this long-term mode of thinking, even if we are likely to be rewarded handsomely in the end. Exponential growth does not get the attention it deserves from most of us. Many of us don't have that sort of patience. When's the reward? Forty years from now? I'll worry about that later.

Multiplying money is very much like playing physical sports. Not many of us say, I think I'll start playing tackle football when I'm 50. Let me start pole vaulting when I turn 60. I'll take up gymnastics at 70. Boxing sounds like a good pastime to look into once I'm retired. But we do put off saving until ages where we're not as fit for it. Olympic gymnasts can be at their peak around age 16. Olympic ice skaters average around 22 years of age. The average age of an NFL player is 26.

We are told we should start saving early, save when we're young, or save for a long time. But this can be a slightly unproductive generality. There's not a better way to be so unspecific about something holding so much latent potential.

If a track coach realizes mid-race that her athlete is likely to win, she should not fail to encourage her runner with great exertion that it is possible to take the gold. This is no time for relaying only mildly encouraging messages. If a baseball coach is waving a runner to round third base and go for home while the ball is still being recovered in the outfield, he should do so with an appropriate level of intensity, intensity that matches the moment. Or what about an athletic team that is brimming with raw talent, enough to win championships, but is never given direction to put that talent to proper use?

Likewise, most of us have plenty of multiplying power but have not been coached on how to put it to use. We have no one encouraging us to do so. Let me run a few commonly heard financial suggestions by you, and you tell me if you get excited by them.

Save 15% for retirement.
Excited? No? Okay.

Save early to take advantage of compound interest.
Still not excited?

Have 10 times your salary saved up by the time you're 65.
No excitement yet again?

The following chart, "Multiplied Dollars," is the above statements in visual form. It's the traditional chart showing how invested money grows over time. It graphically states that the longer we save, the more money there will be later. It's a later-minded chart. Save now. Not much happens for a while. Practice patience.

The reward comes later. It's the ultimate graph showing delayed gratification. Seeing this visual motivates some people to take action, but it does not inspire most.

Following the same marshmallow-multiplying effect from the last chapter, this chart is a visual of that phenomenon. In graph form, we see that an input of money at age 22 can multiply by 16 when we retire 40 years later at age 62—so an input of $1,000 would multiply to $16,000.

Multiplied Dollars

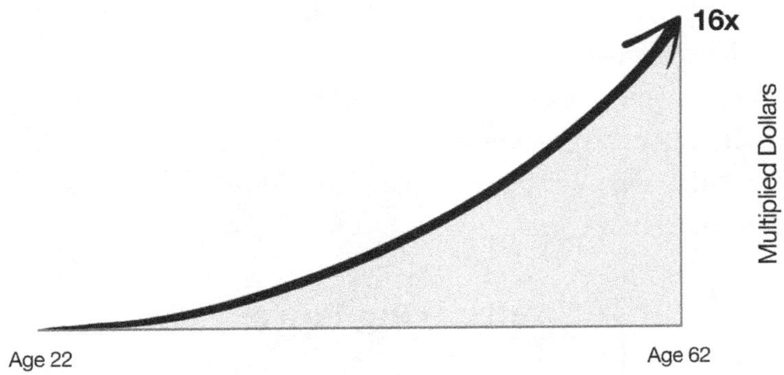

Despite the fact that money-multiplying speeds up and becomes extremely fast in those latter years, getting a glimpse of that curve still hasn't been enough to get the lot of us to take advantage of it. Exponential thinking is not intuitive—linear thinking is. We have a hard time believing that exponential growth with money truly even occurs. It feels a lot more like magic, not like it's grounded in reality. It feels too good to be true.

If most of the population is now-minded, and most of us can't stand the fact that financial gratification is delayed until years in the future, then we need to consider speaking in now terms.

FLIP THE CHART

Our human psychology may very well be working against us, preventing us from setting aside funds now. So what do we do about this? If we know a majority of us are unmotivated to slowly amass money, we need to flip our thinking. And when we do, that can reveal a new thought to us—a simple, under-our-nose-the-whole-time answer. Flipping the chart then changes to show us what our money-multiplying power is *today.* It says, "I have the most multiplying power now—right now." It speaks in today terms. It takes later-minded and turns it into now-minded.

See below how we start at age 22 with a multiplying power of 16 with our money. When we flip the chart in this way, it becomes about an ability we own. It's about us. We wield that multiplying power. This chart gives us ownership over an ability we currently have rather than a dollar we'll gain later. That's much more real. That's much more "now."

Multiplying Power

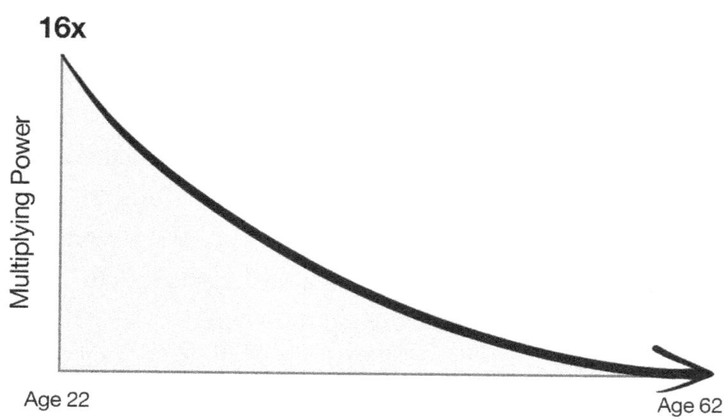

OUR SUPERPOWER

Let's just put it plainly. We have a superpower. That's right, we do. We have a superpower. We all do. It's called the power of 16. When we're birthed into our career lives, we all have it.

In an average American career, when we start working, we have the multiplying power of 16, shown here at the left of the previous chart. When we invest money, earning a normal rate of return (remember, we're using 7.2% for the purposes of this book), that money multiplies 16 times over our working years—the power of 16.

Knowing we start our careers with the power of 16 is the perfect motivation to save more up front. This should really get emerging workers fired up about how empowered they are. You mean young people have been gifted a unique opportunity to multiply money that they won't have at any other time in their lives? Yup.

AGE DOES MATTER

They say size does matter. Well, in the world of finance, it's not about size—it's all about age. That's right—age does matter. Let's take a look to see how things are from an age perspective.

I've heard things like, "When I get older, I'm going to start investing more," or, "When I get promoted someday, I'll finally have money to spare to save for retirement." These are both damaging thoughts that kick the responsibility for our finances down the road.

News flash: our finances are not a pinecone, empty soda can, or other such object we might kick down said road. The most likely thing the average person will do when we make more money is spend more. We've gone over this previously. It's called lifestyle inflation. Make more, spend more, make more, spend more.

So, let's demystify the thought that we are better putting off saving until later in life. Yes, we are likely to have a higher income as we get older, but there's a highly misunderstood thing amiss here. The older we are, the less time we're giving our money to grow. We may think we need to develop some investing skills before we start to invest as well. This is also false. For the average person, investing early in life in widely available index and mutual funds can even surpass being studied in finances. In fact, if I could go back to when I started my career, I'd find a way to max out my retirement fund contributions from the get-go! Using our age to our advantage can even beat rate of return, investment type, savvy, and timing the market. Age, not investing chops, is the secret.[8]

OUR WAKE-UP CALL

So, up to this point, we've been merely looking at what happens if we invest money one time at age 22. What happens if we invest more than once in our lives? What if we also invest when we're 32, 42, 52, 62—or what if we invest all the years and paychecks in between? Well, the answer is that we'd really be leveraging our multiplying power. Understanding what happens if we invest once at age 22 allows us to focus on the basic concept of exponential growth. We can zoom back out now and look at the effect of investing beyond that.

---

[8] Avoid speculative or overly risky investments.

Multiplied Dollars

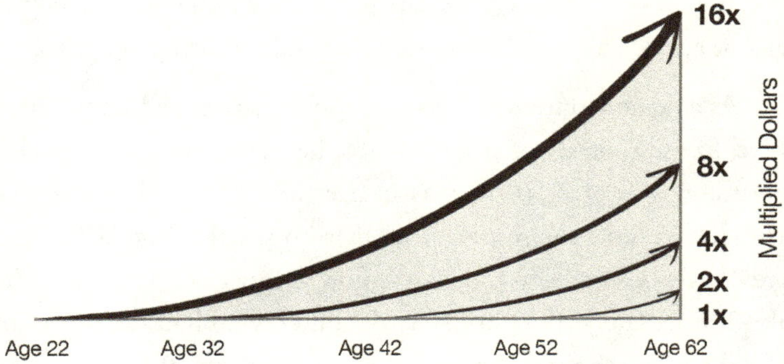

We can see above that if we invest at age 22, that money can multiply to 16 times the initial amount 40 years later. At age 32, money can multiply to eight times the initial amount. At age 42, it can multiply to four times the initial amount. At age 52, two times. And at age 62, that is when we might consider retiring.

Multiplying Power

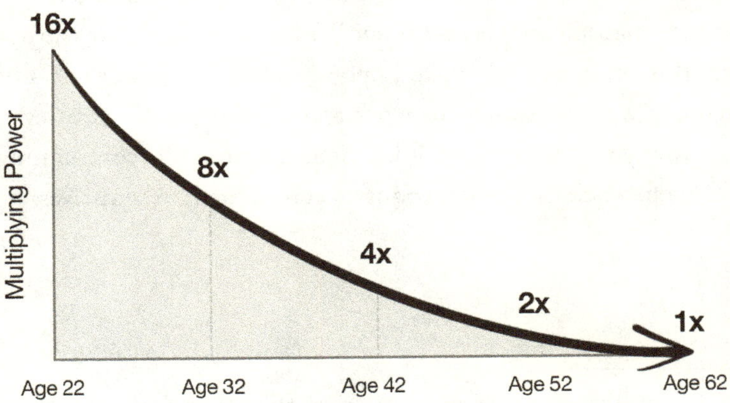

And when we apply numbers to our flipped chart, we see that we have the multiplying power of 16 at age 22. We have the multiplying power of 8 at age 32, the power of 4 at age 42, the power of 2 at age 52, and again, we might consider retiring at age 62.

As a demonstration of how this applies, someone I know came to realize she could potentially double her retirement funds wielding the power of 2, as she was in her early fifties. Having twice as much in our retirement accounts is no small thing! What had previously been a hazy future was now gaining clarity to her. She also immediately thought of her daughter, who had the power of 16. She knew she could help her make good use of that leverage in her twenties. She now had a simple understanding and was putting it into use.

For those of us who want to take this a step further, let's take a look. Say we want to set aside money earlier than we're discussing—say at age 12. We now have the power of 32. *Thirty-two?* Are we serious? The power to multiply our initial investments 32 times? Okay, any young people reading this right now truly do possess a superpower. Can someone hurry up and invent time travel so I can go back and tell my 12-year-old self about this money-multiplying phenomenon? With this principle, we can apply this thinking and expand upon it—there's a power of 64 or more if we start earlier[9] or work and live longer. You can even improve your kids' or grandkids' financial future by contributing for them when they're too young to contribute for themselves.

---

[9] We have the power of 64 at age two, which for most of us would mean having investments made on our behalf. We'll talk about options for supporting your children in this way in chapter 10.

TIME IN THE MARKET

When we talk about age as a major factor in investing, this could also be stated as the number of years we invest for, otherwise known as time in the market. See the kind of multiplying power with money we have here, looking from the number of years we're investing (via a 7.2% rate of return over time):

- **Invest for 10 Years:** Multiplying power of 2
- **Invest for 20 Years:** Multiplying power of 4
- **Invest for 30 Years:** Multiplying power of 8
- **Invest for 40 Years:** Multiplying power of 16

And if we look beyond the typical career duration of 40 years, we can see how multiplying doesn't stop there:

- **Invest for 50 Years:** Multiplying power of 32
- **Invest for 60 Years:** Multiplying power of 64

Things happen slowly, and then they happen quickly. Psychologist and author Angela Duckworth points out that "Grit is passion and perseverance for long-term goals." The very act of investing takes grit, especially in the beginning. We must practice some level of mental fortitude as we invest during the initial stage when results may appear less significant.

But if we agree to run this race, the steps we take in the beginning are not like the steps we take at the end. Look at the first decade of investing in the next grid. One thousand dollars doubles into $2,000—that's $1,000 in growth. But now look at the last decade. Down the road, $8,000 turns to $16,000—an $8,000 increase over the same 10-year span of time. Things start out slowly, and then they happen quickly. And the same goes for multiplying money. The most action happens at the end of the race, and the longer the race we run, the larger the returns are.

Outsized Returns

At this point, you may be getting that tingling feeling, that thing we call motivation—the understanding that if you act early and act now, you can make the biggest impact possible by multiplying the money you steward. The myth of waiting to save for retirement until later in life is now lying on the floor in small, stomped-on smithereens.

WORK 1/16TH AS HARD

The world does not want you to know about your multiplying power because if you knew, you'd stop spending as much!

Let's say you have a choice of gigs. For one gig, you can get paid $1,000, and you'd need to work 16 hours to earn that amount. Now let's say, for another gig, you only need to work eight hours for the same amount. Easy choice, right? Now how about four hours...two hours...one hour. One hour! One hour of work for the same amount! Wouldn't you choose that gig? You've got family to spend time with, hobbies to engage in, and sleep to do. Of course you'd sign up for higher pay for fewer hours worked. But do we?

In the initial scenario of working 16 hours, we're earning $62.50 an hour. In the scenario requiring one hour of work, we're earning $1,000 an hour. Do you see the difference?

Now, let's take this concept of doubling and see it from different angles.

What if we could work 1/16th as many hours? Instead of a 40-hour workweek, we'd work two-and-a-half hours a week.

Let's say instead of having to carry a load 500 feet, you only have to carry it 31.25 feet.

Or instead of buying something for $100, it instead only costs $6.25.

You see, that's what it's like to have the power of 16. When I am 62 years old, I need to work multiple times harder just to get the same resulting dollar amount that my 22-year-old self could.[10] If I decided I wanted to have $1 million by age 62 while I was in my twenties and started saving then, I'd only need to save up $62,500 by age 22 for it to multiply by 16 times and turn to $1 million by age 62. But if I waited until age 62 and suddenly decided that I wanted $1 million, I would need to save the full million and work for every single dollar. An hour's work for an hour's pay. That's working multiple times harder. Not 5% harder, not 10% harder, not even 100% as hard—over 1,000% harder.

The world tells us if we save now, we'll have lots later. The problem with this is that it asks us to be later-minded. Statistically, we're not later-minded people. We're now-minded. Exponential thinking is leverage. Ever try picking up a boulder with your back? Don't do it! But if a strong plank of wood is properly wedged under a stone to create a lever and fulcrum, stepping onto that plank can move a rock otherwise too large to move by hand. Work gets done easier with leverage. That's the point. We don't have to work

---

10 Inflation will play a part in lessening the value of the dollar over time.

long or hard to get the exact same output with the money we manage.

Now we're ready to dive deeper into understanding how our multiplying power adjusts over time by exploring Financial Epiphany #3: Exponential Potential.

Chapter Review:

Financial Epiphany #2: The Power of 16

- **Flip the Chart:** Traditional financial thinking requires us to be future-minded. When we flip our thinking, we force money to pose in a now-minded way, revealing our multiplying power.
- **Our Superpower:** At age 22, we have the power of 16—the ability to multiply money by 16 times.
- **Age Does Matter:** When we begin working, this is the time to activate our superpower with multiplying money. This is a more powerful and leveraged time to save aggressively than when we're older, even if we will potentially have a higher salary later in life.
- **Our Wake-Up Call:** What happens if we invest on an ongoing basis, or even earlier in life? There's a multiplying power of 32 and 64!
- **Time in the Market:** Another way to look at the multiplying power of money is by looking at how long you invest for rather than looking at age. This comes in handy if you work more or fewer years than is typical.
- **Work 1/16th as Hard:** When we are in our 60s, we need to save 16 times more than when we are in our twenties to arrive at the same dollar amount.

Action Items:

Financial Epiphany #2: The Power of 16

- **Identify Your Multiplying Power:** The ages 22, 32, 42, 52, and 62 are referred to in this book as part of a simplified approach. For each of the years in between, see the list "What Is Our Multiplying Power at Different Ages?" on page 176 of the appendix. What is your current multiplying power with money?
- **What If My Rate of Return Is Different from 7.2%?:** See how different rates of return multiply money through the chart "How Do Different Rates of Return Impact When We Have the Power of 16?" on page 180 of the appendix.

CHAPTER 7

Financial Epiphany #3: Exponential Potential

Losses hold a greater weight in our psychology than gains. The natural world treats threats as more urgent than opportunities, and there's good reason for that. Say you happen across a serene-looking drinking hole in the Australian outback. What a find. The glistening water calls out to your parched throat after miles of trudging there. But then the hairs on the back of your neck stand up as, from the corner of your eye, you notice the bumpy scales of a crocodile creating ripples in the water.

Avoiding that particular drinking hole could be good for you today. Putting in the effort to hike further to a safer one registers as worth the wait. Better to live another day than to satisfy our immediate thirst and resultantly become someone's dinner.

In 1979, psychologists Amos Tversky and Daniel Kahneman studied loss aversion, explaining it as a cognitive bias that describes how, for individuals, the pain of losing is psychologically twice as powerful as the pleasure of gaining. Is it a predator, or is it not a predator? Weighing the difference properly is good for our survival. Losses tend to loom twice as large as gains.

Back in the world of money, our multiplying power lessens as we age. That's a perceived loss. The classic saying is "use it before you lose it." Now, that's a good use of our pessimism regarding losses. We can choose to use our pessimism constructively, redirecting us toward positive change, harnessing it. Take, for instance, the Japanese martial art judo, which practices throws and grappling techniques using an opponent's strength, weight, and movement against them. Judo means "gentle way," so those who use it are thought of as practitioners of the gentle way. They learn to redirect their opponent's force and use it to their advantage rather than trying to overpower them with their own strength. Through this approach, a weaker opponent can beat a significantly stronger opponent.

Similarly, we can use the strength behind our pessimism to work for us. Our money-multiplying power diminishes steadily over time? Well, let's use that fact to invest now before our multiplying power goes away entirely.

Let's be decisive. Let's not be afraid to try new things, make decisions, and push ahead. A wait-and-see approach will, in this case, leave us behind. Sarah Frances Brown put it this way: "Twenty years from now you will be more disappointed by the things you didn't do than by the ones you did." So take action. Activate yourself. Awaken your financial giant. As author and inspirational speaker H. Jackson Brown Jr. put it, "There's nothing more expensive than a missed opportunity." Choosing not to take action can translate into actual missed dollars, so he is literally right!

Even if we feel like we've missed a train, we are not alone, as most of us share in that feeling when it comes to personal finance.

G. K. Chesterton, a prolific writer, humbly admits, "The only way of catching a train I have ever discovered is to be late for the one before." Have we missed a train? Let's get on the next one.

LISTEN TO OUR ELDERS

Pretty consistently, through surveys and interviews, older generations are admitting, "I wish I had saved more earlier." So let's do that. Let's save more earlier. Listen to what they are saying. And consider who you will become—them! Sixty percent of retirees wish to plan their retirement differently than they had, with the biggest mistake being not saving with more intent earlier in life.

Inevitably, we will all have a need for retirement income, so why not do now what current retirees are imploring us to do from their vantage point? We have a chance to take action with money while we still have the power to do something about it. If we do now what we'll want later, when later comes, we'll already have been doing it. It's like deciding we want to win a race, and before we know it, we're crossing the finish line because we've already been running it for years.

Although it's not completely devoid of risk, the risk of taking action and putting money in a retirement account is much smaller than the risk of not doing so at all. There is a guaranteed loss if we fail to start. By not inviting money the chance to multiply, we are locking in losses from the get-go. That should be enough motivation to get us to take action and reroute our overspending. Now we can make sacrifices, looking at how quickly our multiplying power goes away over time.

EXPONENTIAL DECAY

Just the sound of the term *exponential decay* makes me want to cringe. If it rubs your ears the wrong way, that's a good sign. Exponential decay explains what is happening to our multiplying power over time. Our multiplying power is halving. In our Simple Framework,[11] it's being cut by 50% regularly every 10 years.

The time it takes for our multiplying power to reduce by half is aptly called its half-life. The term *half-life* is commonly used in the field of pharmacy where it describes the time it takes for a drug's initial potency to be reduced by half after it's been ingested and is circulating in the body.

Yes, our money-multiplying power gets cut in half, then in half again, then again and again—four times over our working careers if we labor the average 40 years. Sobering? Don't feel bad, because we all share this path.

I've never spoken so positively about looking at things negatively. But loss aversion is our friend here. It's here to help, just like pain exists to help us. Without pain receptors, our bodies may not notice a burned finger, a sprained ankle, or an achy body suffering from an infectious virus. Pain has a purpose. Its function is to protect us so we may act. "Ouch, that hot stove hurts, so I'll retract my hand." "I can't bear to walk on my injured foot. Well then, I'll elevate my ankle and ice it." "My whole body is achy and I'm getting chills. Time to consider staying indoors and sleeping it off."

Experiencing pain can lead to action. And knowing that our money-multiplying power is cut in half every 10 years is meant to cause just the right kind of discomfort to lead to action.

---

[11] Simple Framework: Starting a career at age 22, working 40 years, investing for a 7.2% rate of return.

DO NOT SQUANDER YOUR SUPERPOWER—UNLEASH IT

Let's say we could choose to wield the power of a superhero. For some of us, that power might be flying, or X-ray vision, or super strength. Let's take a look at flight, for one. Imagine we have the option of flying high in the sky amid the clouds. Commuting is no longer an issue. We're up and over buildings like it's nothing. Now, if we apply the rule we're discussing, our ability to fly halves every 10 years. So, say a decade passes, and we can't reach the clouds anymore. Well, at least we can fly to the top of a building. After the next 10 years, our flying ability halves again, so we can reach a few floors up. Pretty impressive still. Well, after the next decade, our flying ability gets us up to the gutters of our house, so we can clean without a ladder. Not bad—the neighbors are still jealous.

The trouble is that most of us sit on our superpower. We don't use it or fully take advantage of it while we have it. We use it hesitantly, sparingly. We allow the company we work for to take the helm by meagerly auto-increasing our 401(k) contributions. Where's the boldness in that? We start using our superpower at the end of its life when it's already fizzling out. When we could soar through the sky, we settle for relying on Social Security checks.

When we start our careers, the debt products being thrown at us left and right at that time are like kryptonite—and we go ahead and shackle ourselves with them willingly. *Forget flying. I'll relinquish my potential by getting into debt, and others can divvy up the power I've been bestowed.*

We are holding something timely in our hands that we need to take advantage of. Can you imagine being gifted a brand-new computer and claiming, "I'm going to wait 10 years before I start using this?" It's lost more than its pizzazz by then. Will it even turn on? How about a cell phone? Do we set it aside and wait a dozen years to begin using it?

As we grasp an understanding of our money-multiplying power, a shroud has been lifted. If we save, it is no longer going to turn into a mystery amount years from now—a blurry image barely recognizable through a rusty telescope. We now clearly see the multiplying power we have. Call it our exponential potential, our capacity for multiplying money. Referring to our Simple Framework, at age 22 we have the multiplying power of 16, the ability to turn $1,000 into $16,000. That's incredible! Ten years later, at age 32, our multiplying power halves to eight. At age 42, our multiplying power is four. And at age 52, we can multiply our money by two.

It's sobering to see we have a diminishing chance of multiplying our money as we age. It's prudent to keep in mind that most of us will retire in our early 60s, whether we like it or not, due to health issues with ourselves or family members. Or we might experience potential layoffs, downsizing, or employment-related issues. Better to not bet on a game where the odds are against us. Using our exponential potential is betting on a game that is in our favor.

OPPORTUNITY COSTS

There's a saying, "Most people miss opportunity because it is dressed in overalls and looks like work." Well, if we've previously overlooked our financial opportunity, we have a second chance now. Carpe diem! We can seize the day—or, in this case, seize our financial opportunity before it diminishes.

With all this talk of opportunity, just what is an opportunity cost? In the case of the children involved in the marshmallow test a couple of chapters ago, an opportunity cost is realized when the child chooses to eat a marshmallow immediately, thus forfeiting additional marshmallows in the future. The child handed in the opportunity to earn free marshmallows by cutting off the marshmallows' chances to multiply.

Opportunity costs nip what we have in the bud, cutting our future short by gobbling things up today, indulging in instant gratification. And in the end, we won't have much of a harvest. We face choices every day about where we're putting our dollars. If each dollar I spend now has the power to multiply 16 times if I instead invest it, do I really want to be spending it now?

We deserve to enjoy the money we earn, purchasing and providing for our needs, but we Americans are scandalously poor at stopping there. Do I want the latest, buzziest car now, the one whose car payments will put monthly financial strain on me? Or do I buy a used car now and set aside the extra cash to grow so I can purchase the cars I need over the rest of my life with more relative ease?

> *"Instant gratification lasts a day, but financial wellness is gratifying every day."*

You see, if we do the smart thing now, we reap the benefits later. These are hard things to make up later in life. Instant gratification lasts a day, but financial wellness is gratifying every day. There is great freedom awaiting us.

WHAT ALBERT MAY HAVE HAD TO SAY ON THE MATTER

Albert Einstein is said to have admired this sort of money-multiplying phenomenon. Now, although he likely did not make an official statement on multiplying money, we have to love that history has attempted to attribute the thought to him and add gravity to the matter. Thinking along those lines, if one of the most celebrated minds of all time is associated with the multiplying of money, then it must be an intelligent thing to do!

We've been using the terms *multiplying money* or *exponential potential*, but its results go by another name as well: *compound interest*. Compound interest is an old term. It's a banker's term. But, to many today, it's not a term that evokes a soft, cuddly feel. It's cold, hard, has sharp edges, and is about as comfortable as hugging a cash register.

Likely with a hint of humor, Einstein has been unofficially credited with the saying, "Compound interest is the eighth wonder of the world." The eighth wonder of the world? On par with the Egyptian pyramids or the statue of Zeus at Olympia? That's a bold comparison. The Great Pyramid of Giza alone stands 455 feet tall, has a footprint of 566,286 square feet, and is formed from 2.3 million blocks. But unlike possessing an ancient pyramid or a 40-foot tall statue made of gold and ivory in our backyard, we actually can own and wield compound interest for ourselves.

Picturing those awe-inspiring wonders reminds me of a neighbor of mine, Frank. Frank custom-built his own full pipe organ in his living room, complete with thick wood frame, rows of golden pipes lined up vertically, and two sets of keyboards. It took him three and a half years to build, and there was no guarantee it would work once completed. Do you know anyone with that sort of focus, determination, and faith?

Well, the finished pipe organ did in fact work. He told me that when people came over and saw the musical monstrosity taking over his living room, he noticed some would not allocate a moment's notice to it, entirely ignoring its presence. Wonderful things such as Frank's pipe organ may not always receive the attention they deserve, but an even greater misfortune is missing the opportunity to acknowledge and participate in the marvel of compound interest. So why hasn't compound interest struck us as amazing and impressive as it's purported to be?

If Einstein, known as one of the most intelligent human beings of all time, is popularly said to endorse compound interest as one of the greatest opportunities of our lives, why haven't we been convinced to take better advantage of it? Shouldn't we be using it, studying it, and applying it into our lives to the greatest degree possible? It's something that is available to all of us, yet most of us only tap into a fraction of its potential.

The rest of Einstein's alleged quote reads, "He who understands it earns it. He who doesn't pays it." The pages we've read up until now have focused on just these very two things: grasping the concept of compound interest to empower ourselves to earn it. And, conversely, we've learned to steer clear of debt, which is actually paying compound interest to those we owe. That lender is filling their coffers when we pay those associated interest payments to them, shifting our multiplying power from us to them.

What we have here is a life-altering concept that has been

overlooked. It's our exponential potential, our ability, which diminishes over time, to multiply money. We now recognize what a treasure it is and how important it is to use it with fierce intentionality. And now from here we'll go over how to set up a money-multiplying machine for ourselves.

Chapter Review:

Financial Epiphany #3: Exponential Potential

- **Sense of Urgency:** We have our greatest multiplying power right now. Don't wait!
- **Listen to Our Elders:** One of the main regrets retirees share is that they didn't save more money and start earlier.
- **Exponential Decay:** Our ability to multiply money starts out the strongest it ever will be, and it typically diminishes by half every 10 years.
- **Do Not Squander Your Superpower—Unleash It:** Put your ability to use while you have it. You are empowered. Time to act!
- **Opportunity Costs:** These occur when we purchase something now rather than investing those funds that can grow, affording us much more in the future.
- **What Albert May Have Had to Say on the Matter:** Albert Einstein is said to have called multiplying money, also known as compound interest, the eighth wonder of the world, which can lead us to recognize how powerful it is.

Action Item:

Financial Epiphany #3: Exponential Potential

What Will Your Multiplying Power Be in the Next Decade?: If you plan to continue working, compare what your money-multiplying power is now to what it will be a decade from now. How about a decade after that? Look ahead and get a feeling for how your multiplying power halves every 10 years. See the list "What Is Our Multiplying Power at Different Ages?" on page 176 of the appendix for an easy reference.

STEP 4

Taking Action

Learn what to do, then do
what you've learned.

Chapters:

CHAPTER 8

Let's Set Up Your Money-Multiplying Machine

I once had a legacy garage. By *legacy*, I mean it had generations of junk that had been passed down to me. Old tables, shelving that held rows of items that hadn't moved or been seen in years, cans of dried paint, tools strewn throughout different drawers, bottles of randomly saved bolts and straightened nails. Hordes of items lay there collecting dust and taking up space.

I dreaded looking for a tool in that garage. Sometimes I'd sit in place, thinking about how unpleasant it would be to look for something I needed. In fact, I often preferred to make the trip to the hardware store to buy a new tool rather than sift through the entire garage for a tool I already owned, just to avoid searching for a needle in a haystack and feeling the resulting disappointment of potentially turning up empty-handed.

I overcame this major pain point in my life, spending two weeks revamping the garage. It took three trips to the dump with my brother's pickup truck, followed by acquiring rows of heavy-duty shelving and determining that each tool and item had a place. Garage life became much better. Now if I need a tool, I know whether I have it and exactly where to find it, and I go directly to it when I need it. It's kind of a life-changer to take that sore spot in my life and turn it into something functional that brings me some element of satisfaction. I committed to those two weeks of hard work, and now I can enjoy the fruits of my garage makeover from here on out.

Taking the time to set things up is worth it, and this applies even more for our financial life and future. The effort we put in now can ripple across all the remaining years of our lives, removing pain points and replacing them with financial progress. So, let's jump in and discuss the main tools we'll need to set up to multiply money.

WHAT ACTION TO TAKE

In the following chart, you can see various locations we can park our money to grow. The first three we'll talk about are popular options capable of multiplying money in the way we've been discussing. That includes the retirement options: the 401(k) or 403(b) plan,[12] if either plan is available to you at your workplace, and the IRA. We'll also cover brokerage accounts, which are also capable of multiplying money along the lines we've been discussing.

The remaining options are better for short-term use and make it easier to access our money. Although they are great tools to have

---

12 The 403(b) is available to some employees in public schools, nonprofits, and other sectors. There are many similarities and some differences between 403(b) plans and 401(k) plans; however, for simplicity, we'll continue on by referring to 401(k) plans from here.

in our everyday financial arsenal, when they are shown in the following chart and compared, it becomes apparent how much more powerful and leveraged the first three options are for multiplying money. They really are in a league of their own.

Comparing Account Types

	Rate of Return	Time Horizon	Tax-Advantaged	Company Matching
401(k)	●	●	●	●
IRA	●	●	●	
Brokerage	●	●	◓	
CD / Money Market	◓	◓		
Savings	◓			

In this chart, a fully filled-in circle indicates that the financial vehicle listed may have a benefit or advantage in the long run in that area compared to other options. 401(k)s, IRAs, and brokerage accounts have the potential for relatively high rates of return over time when allocated toward growth investments, but they can also carry the risk of loss. A half circle represents a partial or low benefit/advantage in general, depending on market conditions. This chart uses basic icons to satisfy our simplified approach to learning.

THE 401(K)

Why is the 401(k) America's go-to savings tool currently? Well, this favored retirement savings plan features all four advantages listed in the chart above. Investments within it can offer a healthy rate of return over the long run, the plan takes advantage of multiplying money over time, and it has options to defer tax or grow tax-free.

Employers can also opt to match what we put in, thereby adding in free money from the get-go. If we're excited about earning money in the market, we should be ecstatic about these employer contributions. It's complimentary money, guaranteed and typically paid up front.[13] That can't be beat. The company-matching aspect of 401(k) plans is a powerhouse of a way to multiply money by injecting more on top of what we personally invest. A bigger input can lead to a bigger output.

Typically, what's inside a 401(k) is a bundle of stocks and bonds in the form of index funds or mutual funds. Selecting an index fund that tracks the S&P 500[14] is a great place to start if one is available. A target date mutual fund that adjusts as we age is an option as well for those desiring a hands-off approach.

These benefits and the plan's relative simplicity earn the 401(k) a place squarely on our podium with a gold medal around its neck. Over 60% of employers across the nation offer 401(k) plans. Supported by the U.S. government through tax advantages and a regulatory framework, the 401(k) is hard to compete with as the top retirement savings vehicle of choice.

---

[13] Most employers match employees' contributions each paycheck. Some employers pay a single lump-sum payment annually.

[14] The Standard & Poor's 500 is a stock market index that measures the performance of 500 of the largest publicly traded companies in the United States. It is a key indicator of the overall condition of the U.S. stock market and is one of the most widely followed stock indices. Ask a financial advisor if a market capitalization-based fund or an equally weighted fund might be a good fit for you.

THE IRA

Next is the IRA, listed as second in our previous chart, earning a silver medal. The IRA checks off three of the four advantages that a 401(k) does: offering the possibility of a healthy rate of return, using a long time horizon, and having valuable tax advantages. Like the 401(k), an IRA can consist of index funds and mutual funds, but the IRA can also include an even wider array of options less popular in 401k plans, like exchange-traded funds (ETFs). A popular form of the IRA is the Roth,[15] which allows an individual to use after-tax dollars to invest and grow retirement savings tax-free.

The IRA is the friend of the masses. While 401(k)s are commonly available as a benefit companies either choose to offer or don't, the IRA is an advantageous tool most working individuals have access to outside of their employer. There are contribution limits that do occasionally adjust upward over time, so get familiar with what the Internal Revenue Service allows you to place in annually. For the savvy saver, it's possible to invest in both a 401(k) and an IRA each year.

BROKERAGE ACCOUNTS

A brokerage account is listed third on our chart as an option to multiply money, awarded with a bronze medal. It has some of the same benefits as a 401(k) or IRA—assets within it can achieve a rate of return based on the market, and it uses time to compound and grow. Gains from such an account can be taxed at a somewhat advantaged lower capital gains rate if the assets are held for over a year.

15 Check what the latest income limits are for contributing to a Roth IRA.

Very much like with 401(k)s and IRAs, it's common to hold index funds and mutual funds in a brokerage account. A wide range of other investment options are available for those interested. Popular brokerage firms to contact to start brokerage accounts are Charles Schwab, Vanguard, and Fidelity Investments.

CERTIFICATES OF DEPOSIT AND MONEY MARKET ACCOUNTS

The next account types we'll discuss serve our more short-term needs in life. It is telling to contrast them against the first three account types discussed. They should be an arrow in our quiver, but they are missing some of the crucial advantages that a 401(k), IRA, or brokerage account provide. We'll discuss them for context and comparison, but these accounts usually cannot match the long-term returns the previously discussed vehicles are known for; thus, they won't be options we refer to for multiplying money.

Certificates of deposit (CDs) and money market accounts[16] are offered by banks. They have an element of stability with their returns. When we place money in these vehicles, down the road, we'll receive the money that is due to us. With risk comes reward—so, with the safety these accounts provide, the return is generally less than the return we see from our other stated routes. Time does not serve as much of a benefit in this case, as both are prioritizing making our funds liquid and available. Saving up for a down payment on a house? Keeping money in a combination of these accounts may be right for you. Placing an emergency fund in a money market account can work well.

---

[16] Not to be confused with money market funds, typically offered through brokerage firms.

SAVINGS ACCOUNTS

Savings accounts are available through brick-and-mortar and online banks. Typically, online banks will carry higher interest rates than physical locations. This form of savings ranks last in our list of tools for multiplying money. The rates of return offered by savings accounts may be temporary, as they follow the Federal Reserve's federal funds rate and the monetary policy that the Fed determines, which flows with the ups and downs of the economy.

Traditionally, the returns earned from savings accounts are found to be fairly paltry. Some banks have offered as low as a 0.01% interest rate. With that rate, it would take over 7,000 years to double an initial investment. Savings accounts are not a reliable tool for multiplying money—they serve better as a temporary storage of cash for readily available use.

AUTOMATE YOUR SAVINGS

Steve Jobs, cofounder and former CEO of Apple, was known for his iconic style of dress consisting of a black turtleneck paired with blue jeans. He wore nearly this same outfit every day in order to decrease time and effort spent on the daily task of making clothing-related decisions, which added little value to his day. Precious time was freed up to focus on what he considered more valuable: the pioneering of new technologies.

Managing finances can take a lot of time and occupy a lot of space in our brains. Simplifying the process, like Jobs did with his wardrobe routine eliminates having to dedicate regular effort toward our finances. And that is the key. So, sign up for automatic payroll deductions to contribute to your retirement plan and consider automation for other appropriate investment options as well.

OTHER TYPES OF ACCOUNTS AND ASSETS

When you start managing your money, having money distributed across a mix of the five investment channels and accounts mentioned can be a solid combination. We discussed the 401(k), IRA, and brokerage accounts and compared them to CDs, money market accounts, and savings accounts. There are more options out there, but the theme here is to start out simple.

So where do pensions fit into all this for those who have them? Fifteen percent of private industry workers are offered this type of retirement plan, which provides a regular income to retired workers, typically paid monthly for the rest of their lives. Because the employer typically manages pension investments, we won't spend time discussing them since we're focused on taking ownership of the portion of our finances that we ourselves manage. But if you're expecting regular pension disbursements, add those into your retirement equation.

What about real estate, gold, silver, and other available avenues to direct our money? Some of these cases are outside of the ecosystem we're studying here, but if we are able to reliably achieve a 7.2% rate of return without being weighed down by fees, unnecessary volatility, or risk, then we are multiplying our money in line with the ways we've been discussing. Regardless of where we invest our money, always consider risk and run your thoughts by a financial advisor (we'll cover this next). There are further benefits and considerations with every financial option, such as limits on how much we can contribute per year, fees, and investment selection, but once again, the importance is in starting. We can always refine as we go.

CONNECT WITH A FINANCIAL COACH

Do you feel like you need a coach in your corner to guide you through your next steps? If so, consider establishing a connection with a financial coach and set up an initial meeting. A financial coach is a coach for you and your money, someone who can answer your questions, teach you, and fill in your gaps in understanding about the world of personal finance. They will serve as your accountability partner to help instill good behaviors. A guide like this is helpful when you are making a plan to escape the grips of debt. They can provide motivation to start the accounts mentioned in this chapter and encourage you in multiplying money.

FIND A FINANCIAL ADVISOR

Ask your financial coach for their recommendations on finding a financial advisor and their thoughts on how soon to meet with one to receive advice. An advisor can provide more comprehensive financial planning and help manage investments if you so choose. When choosing an advisor, make sure they are a fiduciary, meaning that they have taken an oath to keep you as an investor and your best interests in mind. Consider meeting more than one potential advisor and interviewing them to find someone you are comfortable working with on an ongoing basis. Some will offer free initial consultations. Some are paid by an hourly fee, which can be a good fit if you simply want to stick to being mentored.

Already investing? You can try one of the advisors at the brokerage firm that is managing your money. If they slow down, explain things so you can track the conversation, and pause to answer every question you ask, you have a winner. A good financial advisor cares about your personal financial health and outcome.

Chapter Review:

Let's Set Up Your Money-Multiplying Machine

- **What Action to Take:** We have options with money and investing. Some popular ways to manage our money are via a 401(k) plan, IRA, brokerage account, CD, money market account, and savings account.
- **Automate Your Savings:** Make multiplying money easy and consistent by setting it on autopilot.
- **Other Types of Accounts and Assets:** There is a long list of investment choices the world has to offer. Where you put your money is a personal choice. Always consider the associated risk/reward balance.
- **Connect with a Financial Coach:** Research and meet with a financial coach to help you practice healthy financial behaviors.
- **Find a Financial Advisor:** Discuss your financial goals and investment objectives and ask questions about their approach and services.

Action Item:

Let's Set Up Your Money-Multiplying Machine

A Friendly Guide for Meeting with a Financial Professional: Be prepared so you can have the best possible experience during your first meeting with a financial coach or advisor. Download the *Financial Epiphany* Money Moves guide for pointers, preparations, and a list of questions that will help you get to know your professional and find out what they offer: financialepiphany.com/moneymoves.

CHAPTER 9

Unleashing Our Exponential Potential

Perhaps the three financial epiphanies from the previous chapters have inspired you to consider multiplying the money you manage and leave overspending in the dust. Now we'll use these three principles as our guiding light as we strategically put to use the financial resources from the last chapter. As we dive in, let's quickly review the three financial epiphanies as we apply them to our financial lives throughout the rest of the book:

- **Financial Epiphany #1: Doubling Years:** A single investment of money can double every 10 years.
- **Financial Epiphany #2: The Power of 16:** At the start of a 40-year career, we have the potential to multiply money by 16 times.
- **Financial Epiphany #3: Exponential Potential:** Every 10 years, our money-multiplying power reduces by half.

Knowing our exponential potential can be just enough to push us over the edge to take action because it's a quick and approximate method, giving us an answer on the spot and only requiring limited mental processing. We don't have a calculator to pull out for every money-related interaction we have—that wouldn't be very practical!—but we can carry rules of thumb like this with us everywhere. It just requires a few seconds to work a grade school-like calculation. We now possess power and understanding over big life decisions at our fingertips.

BUILDING UP A SIXTH SENSE

Learning how to use a new tool, such as our exponential potential, takes practice and repetition. We'll start out intentionally using this tool with the goal of being able to naturally apply it in life without thinking about it over time. That's reaching what I call the "feel it" stage. It's like learning to ride a bike—later in life, we feel how to do it without much mental processing, but when we first learn, our brains and bodies juggle all the individual tasks: lift left foot off the ground, start to pedal with right foot, keep hands equally weighted on the handlebars, and don't forget to look for cars! We work to get beyond mentally processing each component of riding a bike and progress to the point of feeling it. Getting to that point records the action in what is called our procedural memory. It becomes an action that is second nature.

And in the same way, we want to be able to know finances. When should we say okay to buying something? What would that money multiply to if we instead invested it? We want to be able to answer these questions for ourselves, to know and feel finances like the back of our hand, to build a sixth sense about money.

So, from here, let's put our exponential potential into practice and apply what we've learned to the different ages and stages of life we've been mentioning. Our Simple Framework—starting a career at age 22, working 40 years, and investing for a 7.2% rate of return—will apply as usual.

OUR TEENS: WHAT DO WE DO?

Our teen years are a crucial time to lay down our financial groundwork. It's not too early to learn about our exponential potential. Even though these early years are a time before we typically start generating any substantial earnings, they're a time when we can make conscious decisions while wielding some of the greatest multiplying power of our lives. What do we do about this pairing of youth with potent multiplying power? We can team up with Mom and Dad on some powerful actions. These actions are mentioned in the sections to come in this chapter.[17]

If you choose to attend college, plan and prepare to be debt-free once you're out of college or as soon as you can. If you can do that, you'll be primed to do some major money multiplying once you are receiving an income with nothing holding you back.

17 See the upcoming sections for ages 32, 42, and 52 to see what action parents can take on their children's behalf.

AGE 22: THE POWER OF 16

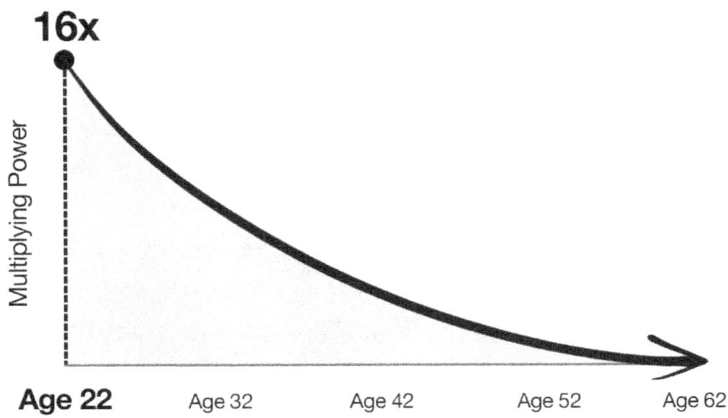

Twenty-two: the age at which we commonly start our careers. This is the most powerful stage of our lives—we are earning a paycheck, and at the same time we possess extremely leveraged multiplying power. From the graph above, we can see that we start with the money-multiplying power of 16 at age 22. This is the time to act! Every $1,000 invested may turn into $16,000 upon retirement. That's $15,000 profit, a 1,500% increase, an opportunity too good to pass up.

Ironically, the importance of this crucial time is a little-known fact. We can breeze right by it and even miss it, focused on school, experiences, and debt. However, our money-multiplying superpower combined with our income is at its most potent at this time! This phase of life is the most critical time to take action.

- **Workplace Retirement Plan:** If you join a company that offers a 401(k) or other workplace retirement plan, opt into it immediately. Did you know that if you max out contributions to a 401(k) for three or four years during this time when you have the power of 16 available to you, that money could multiply into a million dollars at retirement? This time is so crucial that if you work hard and sacrifice now, many of the fruits you'll enjoy later will be able to be traced back to this time. When older or retired folks wish they had acted with conviction, this is the time they are speaking of.

- **Roth IRA:** If a 401(k) is not offered, set up a Roth IRA through a brokerage firm and contribute the maximum you can into it each year.
- **Financial Coach:** Establish a connection with a financial coach and set up an initial meeting. They'll help you understand where you stand financially and instill good behaviors as you start out your career.
- **Financial Advisor:** Interview various financial advisors to find one that is a fit for you. See if they offer free initial consultations or sessions at an hourly rate. Continue to meet or touch base with them once a year, at major life transitions or milestones, or when you need to lean on an expert as you move forward.

AGE 32: THE POWER OF 8

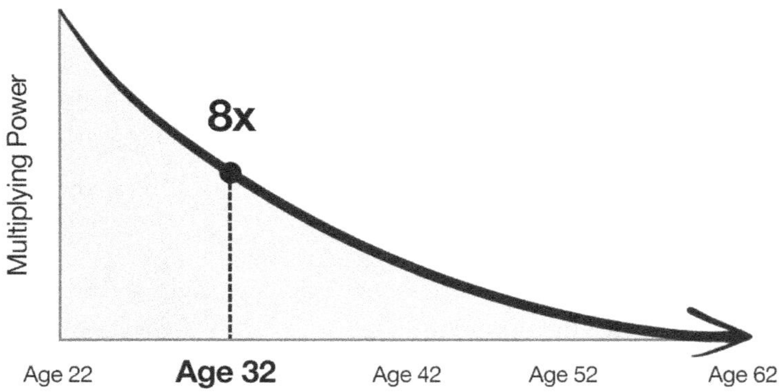

At age 32, we have the multiplying power of 8. Every $1,000 invested can turn into $8,000 upon retirement. We've slid down the curve some, leaving half our multiplying power in the past, but we still have leverage in abundance at this stage of life, with three decades of multiplying ahead of us. At age 32, you may be acquiring a house, welcoming children into the world, or raising a family. If so, congratulations! Momentum in life is building. Here's what to do.

- **Retirement Account Contributions:** If a 401(k) or Roth IRA has been humming along already, keep cranking up what you put in there. If you need help with that, your workplace may offer annual automatic contribution increases to gradually invest more incrementally over time.
- **College Savings Plans:** Get college savings plans,[18] no matter the size, going for each child, and load them up with a nice sum up front if you can. The money you set aside now could grow to be what is needed to cover a good

[18] The next chapter will discuss 529 college savings plans.

part or even all of a college education down the road. You can also consider investing regularly into a college fund with automatic contributions.

AGE 42: THE POWER OF 4

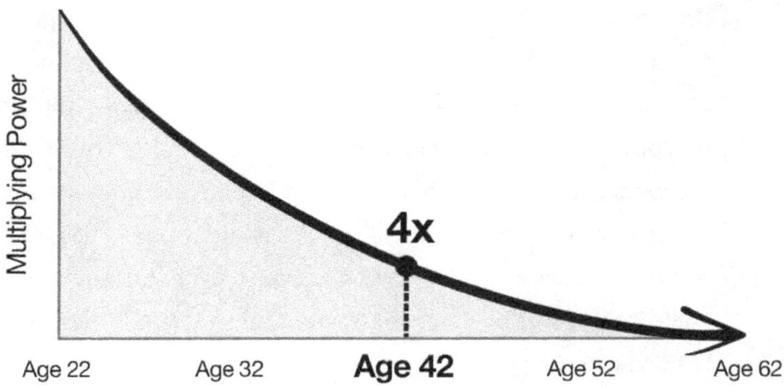

At age 42, we have the money-multiplying power of 4—$1,000 can turn into $4,000 upon retirement. Our curve above is getting a little shallower with its gains, but there is so much good we can do at this juncture. Money can double, then double again. That's a lot of work it's doing for you.

This is the stage of life where we ask ourselves how we're doing. We look back and have enough years behind us to see the results of our choices with money. Hindsight is 20/20. And we really start to care at this point, arriving at the midpoint of our working lives. This happens to be the time we can make an impact on both our own futures and the futures of our children. No kids? How about a niece, nephew, godchild, or other young one you care about? We have the opportunity to teach and lay the groundwork for a future generation and be a voice advocating for good financial habits before the world tries to plant a pattern of overspending in their lives.

- **Retirement:** If your income has grown to allow it, this is a good time to begin putting as much as you can into a 401(k) from here on out. Max out your contribution if possible. Even if you just make a one-time infusion, with the power of 4, injecting $20,000 in could result in approximately $80,000 upon retirement—a very healthy gain.
- **Custodial Account:** For your kids or the other children in your life, consider starting up a custodial account[19] at a brokerage firm and place some of their birthday or gift money into it each time those occasions occur. You may wield the power of 4 at your current age, but they may wield the power of 32 at their age, and that sort of leverage is hard to pass up.
- **Brokerage Account:** For those positioned to, now may be a time to think about seeding a fund separate from a retirement account. This account can be used for your home business, to donate from, or for any other reason. There will be more on what we call the forever fund in the following chapter. With 20 years left to grow, every thousand that's placed in at this milestone may double and double again, leaving you a separate account to spend profits from when you arrive at retirement.

---

19 More on custodial accounts in the next chapter.

AGE 52: THE POWER OF 2

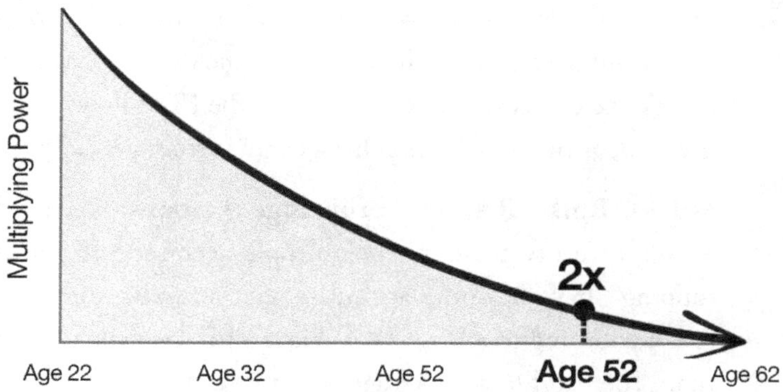

At age 52, we have the multiplying power of 2. Every $1,000 invested can double into $2,000. Doubling money is no small thing, and with the power of 2, we have an opportunity to steward and leverage our remaining multiplying power. Retirement is really starting to come into focus. If you plan to retire in the next decade, your financial advisor will help you determine when to adjust portions of your funds to arrive at a more conservative balance to ride out any market disruptions and lean toward the preservation of all you've been multiplying over the years.[20]

This is the time to guard your future by entering retirement debt-free, so make it a priority to pay off all your debts. If you own a home, work toward having your mortgage fully paid off by the time you step out of those workplace doors for the last time.

- **Catch-Up Contributions:** Here's a secret weapon from the Internal Revenue Service: you can now do catch-up

20 When helping shift money toward preservation, financial advisors may suggest a more conservative approach that may not result in a 7.2% rate of return on investments, which is the rate or return we've been discussing that's associated with doubling investments over a 10-year period.

contributions. Both 401(k) and IRA accounts have their contribution ceilings raised for you at age 50 and after. The amount you place into them can be boosted and is tax-advantaged as well which is the magic behind that gift. Check the current additional amount the IRS allows to be invested, as the contribution limit can rise from year to year.

- **401(k), Roth IRA, and Brokerage Account:** We have an opportunity to invest in multiple accounts. If you're topping off your workplace retirement account, move on to contributing to a Roth IRA. Have you given the max to that? Then add to a brokerage account next.

AGE 62: NOW WHAT?

The pages leading up to this point focus on multiplying money up until age 62. That's a common age for retirement. People choose to clock out their final time for a multitude of reasons: hitting a milestone of working 40 years, saving up enough to live off of, desiring to move on to the next phase of life, freeing up time to take care of grandchildren or aging parents, or stepping out for health- or employment-related reasons.

Maybe you appreciate the stimulation work brings or you need more time for your investments to meet a goal you set. Extending your working years is an option. Continue to take advantage of catch-up contributions to set even more aside for retirement.

Certainly, we should continue to multiply money past the day we are handed our golden watch. However, signing off at work for our final time typically marks the end of keeping our hands out of the retirement savings cookie jar. Your advisor can draft up a custom plan with you, considering your financial posture and life objectives at that point. They will guide you to shift money to be spent, help you with the preservation of a portion of your savings, and point out how much money can be left to focus on multiplying.

THE TORTOISE AND THE HARE: AFTER THE FIRST RACE

In the classic tale of the tortoise and the hare, the turtle treads along slowly but steadily and wins the race. When we are striving to reach the initial financial goal we set for ourselves, we may be sweating over the outcome. *Will I reach the finish line? Will the hare, who has the appearance of a trained athlete, finish before I do?* Many such races were listed out in this chapter, from hitting a retirement contribution goal to funding our kids' college. Other races can include paying off a credit card and finally paying off a home. Life is a lot better after our first finish line is crossed and we pick up psychological and financial momentum on the races that follow.

Forget about the limits we felt as a hobbling turtle—it's as if we've got wings now. Goals start to be achieved quicker and with more confidence compared to the races completed prior. We are adding legitimate trophies onto our shelf. Can we start by exercising steady, turtle-like qualities to get there?

There are so many people—young, old, and in between—who could use an understanding of their multiplying power with money and so many who can do so much good with that power. Unleash that power for yourself. Pick things up at whatever point you're at. Do what you can at whatever age you're at. And don't forget to look at the folks coming up behind you, the younger ones who still have much of their financial futures ahead of them. In what way can you impact them?

Chapter Review:
Unleashing Our Exponential Potential

- **Building Up a Sixth Sense:** This book teaches a rule of thumb: our exponential potential, the multiplying power we own at different milestones in life. It's an ever-present tool we can use when making certain financial decisions.
- **Our Teens: What Do We Do?:** This is the time to lay the groundwork of avoiding debt and freeing up income to multiply.
- **Age 22: The Power of 16:** At this age, we have the multiplying power of 16 with our money. This is possibly the most vital time to multiply money via a retirement account, since at this time we have the combination of both an income and investing leverage.
- **Age 32: The Power of 8:** At age 32, ramp up retirement savings and start up college savings for the next generation.
- **Age 42: The Power of 4:** Max out retirement savings and consider starting up brokerage accounts for your kids and to meet other goals.
- **Age 52: The Power of 2:** Use catch-up contributions to add to your retirement account and prepare to shift some investments toward preservation.
- **Age 62: Now What?:** For many of us, this is the time to retire and enjoy the fruits of our money multiplying. Others can choose to add on years of work, continuing to invest.
- **The Tortoise and the Hare: After the First Race:** Life has many financial races, including paying off various debts and accomplishing financial goals. Momentum is built up with each win.

Action Items:

Unleashing Our Exponential Potential

- **How Much Total Should I Save For Retirement?:** Discover three different methods that will help you triangulate the total amount you should save for retirement. Download the *Financial Epiphany* Money Moves guide to shed some light on your retirement savings goal and find out other moves you can make with your money: financialepiphany.com/moneymoves.
- **401(k), Roth IRA, and Catch-Up Contribution Limits:** Search online for the amount that the IRS allows to be contributed to these retirement investment vehicles for the current year.

CHAPTER 10

Strategic Moves for the Newly Inspired

When our family bought a white Subaru, it was amazing how many white Subarus we started to recognize when we were out. We hadn't detected them before, yet the cars now seemed to be surrounding us in mass frequency. Our attention was attuned to notice them. And just like that phenomenon, as we study money, we can don a set of financial eyeglasses to see the world from a new perspective. Various areas in our lives can start to stand out left and right that we hadn't noticed before, areas we can target and apply our newly minted financial prowess to.

We can create a power to pounce, poised to jump on these financial opportunities as they arise. Be always ready. Be on the offensive, like an athlete who identifies an opening to charge through and score. Football would be a pretty lopsided game if players only attempted to stay in the same place, failing to push the ball down the field, all the while giving up yardage to the opposition. Likewise, can you imagine a game of basketball where an entire team planted itself on just one half of the court, guarding their own hoop in the hopes that their rivals never scored, never taking action offensively?

With that, we'll dive deeper into some tactics to add to your tool belt. Some of these tactics were mentioned in the last chapter, which we'll flesh out along with other tactics to be introduced at this point. And maybe you'll think of your own ways to customize multiplying money in your life from there.

FRONT-LOADING

If someone told us we could make some of our biggest life purchases at 50% of their usual cost, if not less, would that pique our interest? Of course it would. If our past selves had mailed us an envelope containing $10,000 that arrived today, we'd likely be pretty ecstatic, but are we willing to take the actions we need to right now to grow $10,000 for our future selves?

If you like what you've been hearing for these last few chapters, then you'll love front-loading. Front-loading is getting on the financial offensive, and that's probably the most gratifying thing about it. This is our move. This is us empowered. We are choosing to board the financial train, and that train is doing all the huffing and puffing for us. When we reach our destination, we simply disembark, and the money we've invested is there, multiplied, and ready to go!

For my wife and I, the perfect opportunity to try front-loading came when our son entered the world and we realized front-loading could be applied to his college education.

THE COLLEGE FUND

My wife called up the bank to look into a college savings plan for our son, a 529 plan, which provides tax advantages and market growth to money invested for educational purposes. The bank associate asked how old our son was. "Just born this year," my wife responded.

"Oh, you have plenty of time. You don't need to start a 529 plan now," was the less-than-optimal guidance we received. Waiting to invest is the opposite of front-loading. It is completely normal (but occasionally misguided) thinking to claim to ourselves that savings can simply occur later without any ramifications.

When we apply front-loading, we set aside money for a far-off, hefty expense. The bigger the chunk the better, set aside up front, and as early as possible, far from when it's going to be used. That front-loaded money eventually grows on its own to cover a future expense. This is fighting financial fire with financial fire. It's like pushing an empty boat off the dock to sail and seeing it return years later from far-off lands carrying riches galore that are now ours to manage.

Front-loading, in a way, is thinking of the doubling of money in reverse. Financial Epiphany #1 states that money in the market can double every 10 years. So, let's work backward. Say we foresee a looming expense coming 10 years from now. If we save half of the amount we'll eventually need and put it into the market 10 years before we need it, it can double in size to become the amount we desire, all on its own, at an annual rate of return of 7.2%. And all we have to do to make that happen is set that money aside early. Half the money, up front. That's how front-loading works. We set aside half of what we'll eventually need 10 years before we need it. Front-loading is perfectly suitable for long-term savings needs like a child's college education.

Say we'd like to be able to eventually provide our young child $40,000 for his college tuition. Let's view it in grid format.

College Tuition

Child in college
$40,000

Let's say we'd like to start saving 10 years before our child walks onto the college campus. If we set aside $20,000 in a 529 college savings plan, that could double over the 10 years to become the $40,000 we'd need to pay for tuition. See the next grid.

Front-Loading College Tuition 10 Years Earlier

10 years earlier	
$20,000 ▸	$40,000

But wait—we're not stopping there. Say we were feeling particularly proactive before the child was born—before he was given a Social Security number or assigned his first binky. Say that in the middle of the night we thought about our unborn child's financial future and scrambled for our laptop. We elected to sign up for college savings that far up front[21]—for easy math, we'll

[21] A 529 college savings plan can be created under our name, and once our child is born and given a Social Security number, we can name them as the beneficiary at that time.

say 20 years before we plan to pay for tuition. Well, using our rule of thumb, take half of a half, and we would need to set aside $10,000 at that time via a 529 plan. That $10,000 could double into $20,000 after 10 years, and that $20,000 could double into $40,000 just as Junior steps into the lecture hall.

Front-Loading College Tuition 20 Years Earlier

This same scenario would look like the below in graph format.

Front-Loading College Tuition

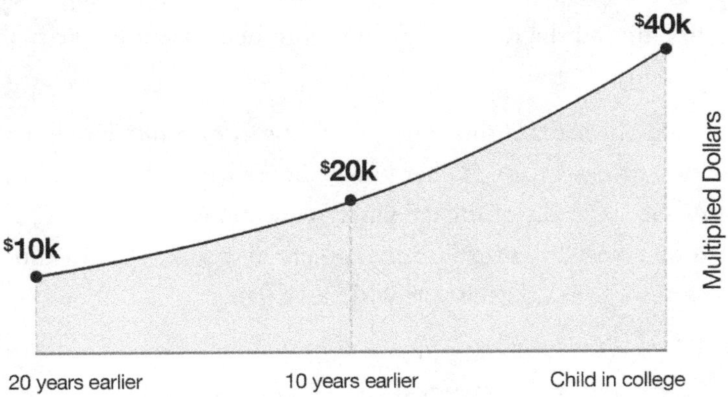

By using front-loading, we are equipped to cover a good portion, or all, of our child's college costs, and we only had to set aside 25% of the final amount to do so if we started near birth.

We gave our money time to double, and double again. Tough to do? Yes. But now we understand how the principle works. Maybe we want to save up for just a certain fraction of college costs. Your call. Want to set aside savings for an eventual grandchild? That would allow even more time on your side to act and grow.

PAYING BEFORE VERSUS PAYING AFTER

This principle starts to really stand out when we look at the fact that the average college student takes out student loans, paying above the asking price of tuition due to the interest paid on the loan. With, say, $10,000 of interest tacked on to an original $40,000 price tag, the cost of taking out a student loan would then be equal to $50,000. That's quite a bit more than the $10,000 cost of front-loading for the exact same education. Compare $50,000 for college after, versus $10,000 up front. Setting aside money around the time our child is born doesn't sound like such bad timing after all.

Once he realized this concept—that money could double and double again—a young father I know immediately started 529 accounts for both his young daughters' educations with confidence. And that is what our exponential potential can do—it can allow us to move forward decisively with our finances.

THE CUSTODIAL ACCOUNT

My wife's parents came over from South Korea, started a dry cleaning business, labored six days a week, and were determined that my wife would never step foot in their business to lend a hand. They decided she would go to college and work a career. They set her up for success. Maybe we, too, feel compelled to bolster others' futures.

It's like setting someone up for an alley-oop in basketball, where a player serves up the ball for a teammate to catch in midair and dunk. Or how about passing the soccer ball to a teammate to get that perfect angle on the goal to score? That's a win for the team. If we're willing to help a teammate out like that, how much more are we willing to do for our own family?

Our kids or grandkids are as far from retirement as they'll ever be, so that means they have the most multiplying years available to them. Economists and financial consultants have posed the idea of baby bonds. A baby bond is a proposal to set aside a certain amount of money for a child at the time they are born. It multiplies on its own untouched over a working lifetime, and when the child grows up and reaches their golden years, a sum large enough to positively impact retirement is ready to be accessed. Sounds phenomenal, right? Well, if top economists and financial advisors are in favor of this idea, what are we waiting for? Are we going to sit around and wait for someone else to determine our family's financial future? Why don't we consider applying this same clever idea ourselves?

Let's run through an example. Say we can muster $5,000 during our child's first years, and we place it into a custodial account. As one option, we can call up a brokerage firm of our choosing and create such an account for our child, naming ourselves as the custodian.[22] Since infants are, on average, around

---

[22] A custodial account is managed by an adult on behalf of a child. When the child reaches the age of majority in his or her state, control of the account is handed over. As another option, ask a financial advisor if rolling over unused investments from a 529 account into a Roth IRA might be a good option.

six decades away from their own retirement age, they possess the multiplying power of 64. So, $5,000 doubles to $10,000, $10,000 doubles to $20,000, $20,000 doubles to $40,000, $40,000 doubles to $80,000, $80,000 doubles to $160,000, and $160,000 doubles to $320,000. That is a gain of $315,000, all starting from an initial $5,000 set aside for the child early on and not touched or added to along the way. Let's view it in grid format.

Front-Loading a Custodial Account

	10 yrs	20 yrs	30 yrs	40 yrs	50 yrs	60 yrs
$5,000 ▸	$10,000 ▸	$20,000 ▸	$40,000 ▸	$80,000 ▸	$160,000 ▸	$320,000

And below is the same multiplying phenomenon in graph format:

Front-Loading a Custodial Account

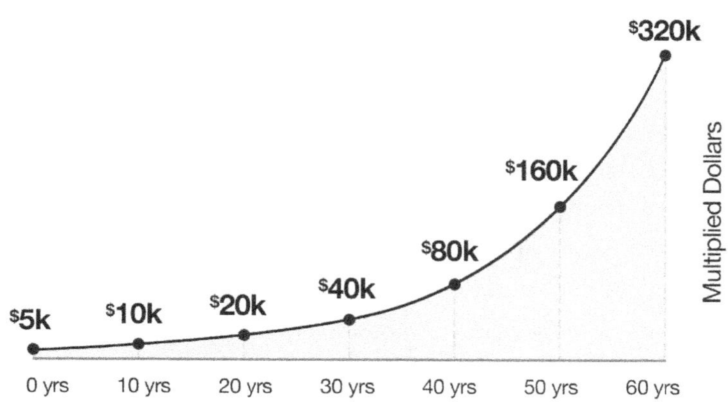

If $5,000 sounds like too much to initiate with, other options include setting aside money more slowly over time or putting in less overall. Readying a nice gift for our kids using such leverage almost sounds like cheating. *Shhh, don't tell them that we didn't work for every dollar!* We set aside just the initial $5,000 investment. That's 1/64th of the final amount. Wow. Doubling money can lead to astronomical results. If our generation does this for the next generation, and the next generation does it for the one after them, we can start to see how planting that initial seed can get a generational wealth ball rolling.

THE FOREVER FUND

Do you run a small business or have a gig on the side? What do you think could happen if you plant a tree that creates a side stream of income that runs forever? The fruit that comes from that fund could potentially help pay for business expenses, taxes, and equipment each year. Let's get into how this works.

Say you set aside $5,000 from your business profits for five years in a row, so you have $25,000 to work with. You start an account at a brokerage firm such as Charles Schwab, Vanguard, or Fidelity Investments, and you inject the money in there, requesting to invest in one or more index, mutual, or exchange-traded funds.

Front-Loading a Forever Fund

Save up for 5 years then invest

$25,000

With money potentially doubling every 10 years, you wait. Twenty-five thousand dollars turns to $50,000, and that $50,000 turns to $100,000.

Front-Loading a Forever Fund and Waiting 20 Years

	10 yrs	20 yrs
$25,000 ▸	$50,000 ▸	$100,000

You come back after those doubling years pass and, with an average 7.2% rate of return on that $100,000 each year from there, that means that going forward you can now pull about $7,200 in returns on average from the account each year. It will be possible to remove annual profits like this for the rest of the time you run the business, and beyond—all without touching the original $100,000 principal. Think about that. Every year after that is now pure gravy, money generated for your business for as long as you please. This is what is referred to when people talk about owning a goose that continually lays golden eggs.

Taking Out Annual Profits from a Forever Fund

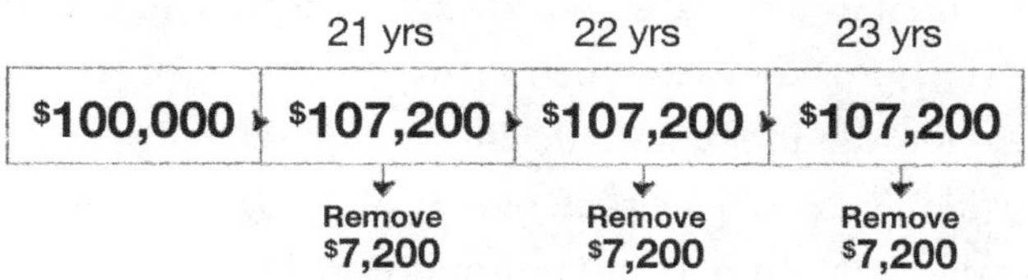

The same idea works for creating a fund to give from. A stash of money can be set aside in a brokerage account that grows to $100,000. At that point, we can pull out an average of $7,200 per year and donate that money to the causes of our choosing, give outrageous tips, or fund nonprofit work. That approximately $7,200 can come out every year from that point forward, with adjustments for market fluctuations.[23] If this sort of money mechanism sounds familiar, it's because it's a common entity in our world today. It's how an endowment works. Endowments are known for funding education, health care, research, social causes, and other such endeavors. We have all most likely benefited from colleges, care centers, or organizations supported by endowments. And if endowments are formed to fund causes in perpetuity, why not borrow from the idea and create one ourselves, no matter the size of principal it holds or the amount of funds it generates? Now that's working smarter, not harder. And just think, what if we planted more than $25,000 initially, or saved up more than $100,000 in the end? Talk about no limits.

---

23 Market fluctuations may create larger than $7,200 returns some years and negative returns other years. Extra money can be left in the account during surplus years, and less or none can be removed during years with negative returns in order to steward the principal amount over the long run.

CREATE A FINANCIAL GARDEN

Let's say we start with a single seed and plant it. That seed has the potential to have substantial benefits, to grow into a tree and bear fruit, provide shade, deliver oxygen, be used as wood to build a house, and even proliferate into other trees that continue to provide all these benefits all over again. It has multiple benefits far beyond its seemingly insignificant initial form as a seed. Our money, if planted properly, can do the same: provide food, comfort, health, and shelter, and proliferate to different aspects of our lives and the benefit of others' lives.

A real estate agent had just finished staging a home and greeted me, the first to drop by the open house she was running. All new light bulbs were inserted in sockets, furniture was perfectly placed, and decorative elements sat on shelves. The place looked its best. I found myself standing in the backyard talking to the agent, and we both peered up at a tree that reached 75 feet into the air, sitting upon a large bank of dirt, like an oversized pitcher's mound. The tree was immovable, sitting directly in the middle of the backyard, a fixture of the property.

The agent mentioned how the seller's son remembered that tree being planted by his father when he was a little boy. And now it was a towering marvel, providing necessary shade to a backyard that was otherwise widely exposed to the afternoon sun, keeping the house cool. The tree had a purpose and had been bringing enjoyment for many years, but it had taken decades to grow.

Think of a garden, one with lush trees supplying an endless amount of benefit for those walking it. In financial terms, each investment account we create is like planting a financial tree. After years of growth, each of these "trees" may bear fruit at any given time, supplying benefits left and right. One may be readying a child for higher education while another hits milestones for retirement. We can watch an account tick up that may one day go toward a down payment on a house for a future generation. Meanwhile, another account grows to the point of regularly covering annual business expenses, and another account becomes ready to hand out donations to support the community.

As we gain understanding of how money multiplies, we can choose to diversify our investment accounts, planting the financial forest that makes sense in our lives to bring forth fruit of various kinds. The fulfillment of a financial goal or the manifestation of a potential blessing may be around a corner at any given time. A garden like this is not meant to spread us thin by starting more accounts than we can handle. We must be diligent in planning our own financial garden that is sustainable in the long run, but discussing it here can show us the possibilities for our finances as we slowly and steadily put our money to the task of multiplying.

By taking the offensive and remaining empowered with our potential to multiply money, we are less likely to be frivolously spending it. Leadership expert John C. Maxwell says it's crucial to keep "telling your money where to go instead of wondering where it went." Our money now has a purpose. It has multiplying to do. It has work to go to. Money is not good at idly sitting around. If we don't save it, it is likely to be spent. It likes to be put to use, for better or for worse. We are less likely to fall into lifestyle inflation when our money has work to do, resisting the urge to increase our standard of living to an unnecessary degree as our income goes up. Focusing on our multiplying power, we're able to maintain the motivation required to make sacrifices and delay gratification.

SIMPLIFYING THE PICTURE

You've survived a lot of graphs and grids over these last few chapters. As much as we've used visuals to help describe some financial and behavioral concepts, we'd be remiss not to run these same graphs through another pass of the simplicity filter we've been applying to everything else in this book. So, let's do just that. Let's continue to simplify.

For some individuals, graphs can create a layer of separation. Like money, they can be intimidating or require our brains to enter a category of thinking we're simply not in the mood for. They can take heavy processing to store mentally—we may worry that we'll lose their details, and along with those details, their relevancy. So, what if we reduced some of the common concepts we've been using down to symbols, an easy instrument to be added to life's tool set, burning a simple image into our minds? Think about how traffic signals or street signs work for us. These simple, easy shapes and representations hold meaning behind them.

Let's start with our multiplying power graph on the following page. We can see that, after we've removed numbers, dotted lines, and textual labels, it easily transfers into the form of a simple downward-arcing arrow. This symbol represents how our money-multiplying power lessens over time.

Multiplying Power

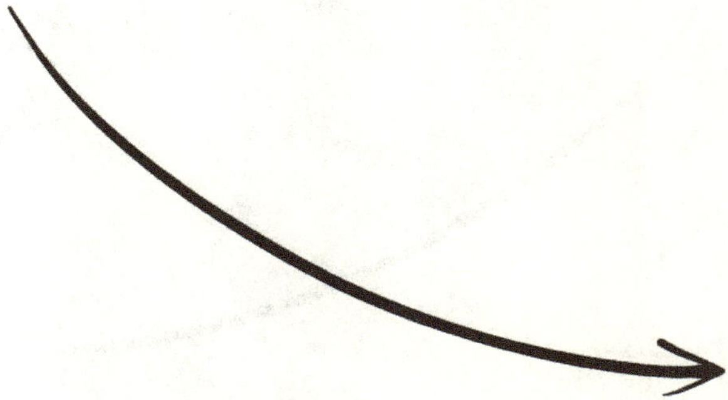

And our multiplied dollars graph? Without the extra labels, it easily takes the form of an upwardly arcing arrow. The shape below represents the gradual growth of our invested dollars over time.

Multiplied Dollars

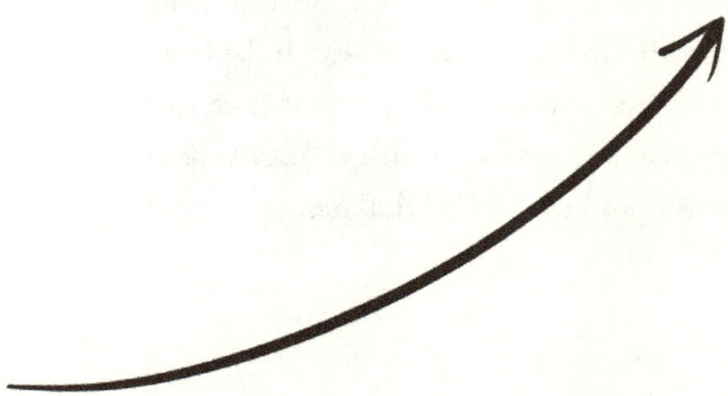

We can combine these two symbols to create a new meaning in our minds. When we superimpose the shapes upon each other, we come up with the following image. These simple lines can speak to us. They show the relationship and causation between our decreasing multiplying power and the resulting multiplied dollars.

Exponential Potential

This relationship is one way of visualizing our exponential potential. The two curved arrows are interdependent. They coexist, like the yin and yang of multiplying money. If we've been actively investing, this shows that, as our multiplying power diminishes over time, our multiplied dollars go up over time.

It's like rolling down one hillside and using that momentum to successfully make it up the next hillside to financial health. Now we have a symbol so simple that it can be efficiently stored in our brains to remind us of this relationship between our multiplying power and multiplied dollars.

Chapter Review:

Strategic Moves for the Newly Inspired

- **Front-Loading:** When you place money in an account early, it can multiply into the amount you'll eventually need later. This can be a great way to seed money toward a college fund.
- **The College Fund:** A 529 plan is a method to use the market to multiply funds, with tax advantages, for your kids' education.
- **Paying Before Versus Paying After:** Investing early to pay for college takes advantage of money multiplying, possibly costing only a fraction of the tuition bill when compared to taking out a student loan.
- **Custodial Account:** We can set up an account to take advantage of multiplying money for others, including our children or grandchildren.
- **The Forever Fund:** An account from which you can remove the profits that were earned each year. Not touching the principal amount allows for this continuous base of money to replenish with investment returns each year.
- **Create a Financial Garden:** Setting up a diversified set of accounts that each have their own unique benefits and goals can allow for money to multiply concurrently for various purposes.
- **Simplifying the Picture:** Simple shapes can be easily remembered yet hold remarkable meaning.

Action Item:

Strategic Moves for the Newly Inspired

Research Offerings at Brokerage Firms: Already have a 401(k) or other existing account at a brokerage firm? Visit their website and look up 529 plans, custodial accounts, and brokerage accounts. No account yet? Try looking up options at Charles Schwab, Vanguard, or Fidelity Investments.

CHAPTER 11

From Products and Prices to People and Purpose

A teammate was the first to tell me this: "If you don't stand for something, you'll fall for anything." And with money, that can be true. Now that we recognize the money-multiplying power we possess, we are on a new set of tracks leading us away from our previous life of spending and debt. We must be diligent and on guard against the host of temptations coaxing us to veer off track. We've already discussed many of them: overspending, taking out debt, keeping up with the Joneses, and lifestyle inflation. These enticements never really go away. They'll always be hovering, increasingly so once we graduate to managing more money.

Once those sums are built up, we may be tempted to take out a loan on our 401(k) or an unnecessary home equity or personal loan, accessing our reserves prematurely to satisfy our desires in the moment. We may be tempted to blow our savings on an impressive new set of wheels, which then require an expansive garage to park in, which then comes with a heavily mortgaged home attached to it. A long road of hard work and commitment can be vulnerable to reversal. Battling these temptations year after year is a challenge. So, let's pull out our next secret weapon to keep our multiplying on course. It's something of an anchor, something that will keep us steady and stable on this new set of tracks over the long haul and lessen the chance of derailment.

OUR PEOPLE-BASED WHY

If our previous challenges dealt with overspending, debt, and the like, we could say our issue was due to products and prices. It's consumerism, giving in to purchases and the instant gratification associated with it all. But really, what is the one thing of infinite value on this planet? People. How do we combine a purpose focused on people with our money multiplying? What is our people-based why?

Let's take a moment, breathe in, and highlight some possible people-based reasons to multiply our money. Maybe your why is one or more of the following things:

- You want to escape debt to bring peace and security to your family.
- You want a healthy marriage free of money problems.
- You want to give your kids the option to go to college.
- You want to be prepared to care for your parents.
- You want to open up opportunities for your grandchildren.
- You want to help out others and your community.
- You want to use money to live out your purpose.

Multiplying money can look a lot different through the lens of each of the above reasons. Any mix of these can serve as an anchor to keep us on track over the years and help us barrel through temptations with our spending. We should aim to have a big why, an overarching why. If we do, we're likely to achieve the goals under it, and our finances will be just one of the objectives we'll fulfill, among others. Paying off a credit card or having another thousand in the retirement account feels much different when it has a deep purpose attached to it. A fully funded retirement account can serve as a great step in the right direction, but it doesn't have to settle in as our final destination. Many of us may spend decades in retirement. So, what is our mission going to be during those decades?

This book is ultimately not about building wealth. That can happen. But what's more important than wealth is (1) not falling prey to the entrapments of debt and (2) being free and empowered to exercise generosity and be available to use finances as one component to help fulfill our purpose, passions, and goals.

WITH GREAT FINANCES COME GREAT RESPONSIBILITY

It's sometimes erroneously alleged that marriage will fix us, that any immaturities, money problems, or hidden behaviors of ours will be whisked away when we tie the knot. Well, all married folks will shoot that fallacy down in a heartbeat, the same way a Super Soaker would a paper napkin. Money problems we've had as individuals become shared with our spouses. What a gift! And the ensuing stress and debates regarding those problems are shared as well. Marriage doesn't fix a person—it only magnifies who we already are. And the same goes for finances. Money doesn't fix us—it only magnifies what is already in our hearts.

Equally erroneous: if we were to win the lottery, would all of our money problems sink into oblivion? Once again, the money behaviors we practiced before guessing those numbers correctly on the ticket are only going to be enhanced for all to see if we receive a big check with lots of zeros on it. More money just multiplies the habits that were already there. If a house, car, boat, and shiny new items come quickly, they are likely only to be lost just as quickly, as many lottery winners discover that their existing mismanagement of money only crashed a bigger plane once that lottery check came in. Many lottery winners eventually go bankrupt within a few years of winning, and they have a higher chance of bankruptcy than the average American.

As we set forth to multiply our money for good, there's also another caution we must take. Like a pendulum, we can swing from one end, deeply wading in debt, to the other end, becoming overly obsessed with multiplying money. What started as a pure motive of escaping debt can lead to overshooting our target, heading overboard in the opposite direction. Life needs balance, so employ discernment here as you proceed forward, and consider mentors, including a financial coach, and safe and appropriate accountability partners to check in on milestones along the way. If your goal is to become wealthy and wealthy alone, this is a good place to slow down and consider the words of this chapter. It can save you a lot of heartache. The principles in this book can lead to unintended results if the accumulation of money is allowed to be at the core of our why. If you don't keep that growth in perspective, the proliferation of the funds you manage can be intoxicating. Seeking money itself can make for a lonely goal and a poor moral compass.

A LIFE LESSON FROM MARKETPLACE DAY

Each student in my elementary school class had weeks to prepare a craft to set up in a storefront in the classroom and "sell" for marketplace cash. We could then turn around and use those dollars, only good in that setting for that day, to buy crafts from other students. It was called Marketplace Day. I worked tirelessly to hand-draw my own line of trading cards. My nine-year-old self felt amused by the drawings and ideas on each card. To my surprise, the other students seemed to agree. In fact, the items were so popular that I never got the chance to close my store to shop the rest of the students' creations. And all the fake money that I stored up selling out of my craft wasn't any good outside of the classroom. It was simply photocopied numbers and pictures on colored paper.

I missed my chance to put what I had earned to use! I left the school that day without the items I had worked so hard to produce, and I didn't have any of the homemade, one-of-a-kind creations from anyone else either. I couldn't even take the fake money with me. I had to hand that back too for use by the school the following year. Talk about leaving empty-handed.

That day as a grade school student taught me a valuable lesson—do not simply store up what you've earned. It can all be taken away. Make financial goals and targets but be generous and be sure to enjoy life along the way while you can.

THE PURPOSE CONTINUUM

When we align ourselves with our purpose, the money we steward can really grow wings. But once again, what will the money we're multiplying be doing when it's all grown up, having undergone exponential growth? We'll have to decide. Money has a way of making us more of who we already are. So, who are we? And who are we times two, times four, times eight, or times sixteen?

The Purpose Continuum Stage #1: Dependency

We can look at our personal purpose across five life stages, which I refer to as the purpose continuum. The first stage in the series is Dependency. If you ever thought the human race was advanced, just try picking up your own head and feeding yourself out in the wild the day you're born. You can't do it. No one can. We have to be fed. We have to be changed. We have to have our dirty bottoms wiped and powdered. We are completely dependent, and our survival is completely in the hands of others. We're not exercising our purpose in life yet, but those who serve us truly are. And that's why the first stage of our life is Dependency.

The Purpose Continuum Stage #2: Learning

Stage #2 is Learning. This season of life encompasses all learning, but in particular schooling from preschool to college and beyond—educating oneself, understanding a concentration, gaining certificates and diplomas, advancing our understanding of the world, and readying ourselves for a job. Our purpose is preparing to be contributors to the economy and society. Never stop learning. Never stop soaking up knowledge.

The Purpose Continuum
Stage #3: Establishing

Now we move on to Stage #3 of the purpose continuum. This is the tricky stage. We may be tempted to stop and reside in this stage, or we can choose to continue our momentum moving forward. It's the Establishing stage. We get a job, move up in our career, get married, get a house, and start a family. We have finally matured beyond our previous two stages to become self-reliant, independent, and justifiably pleased with how things are going. This is the stage where we're busy multiplying money, but that's exactly where we can stay, cycling around and around—gaining, gaining, gaining. Moving up a ladder, going after the next title, acquiring possessions. This is the stage where lifestyle inflation and keeping up with the Joneses are likely to set in. Do we desire bigger purchases, more purchases? Competitiveness and comparison can sneak up on us. We all have our own sticky web here that can halt us from progressing further beyond our own wants, needs, and ambition. I have found myself tangled in these things before. And what if we break free of the many tendrils of the Establishing stage in our lives? What can our money be freed up to do?

The Purpose Continuum
Stage #4: Serving

We can then move onto the fourth stage, Serving. Family, friends, neighbors, and beyond could use our help at times. Is there a favorite cause we can donate to or volunteer with? You may have heard that if we live in the U.S., we're in the top 10% of wealth on the entire planet. World-famous investor Warren Buffett calls it winning the "ovarian lottery" if we happen to be lucky enough to have sprouted our lives in America. As privileged as that may sound, it may sometimes not feel that way. This is where we need to remind ourselves that we are truly fortunate, relatively speaking, and can make it a point to serve others, those in our community and beyond. Is there a way our finances can be used to help when others are in need? Generosity is a great muscle to exercise along our financial journey.

The Purpose Continuum Stage #5: Legacy

Stage #5 is Legacy. What will still be here when we're gone? What will we truly be leaving behind when we're no longer here? It is said that money can work for us, and it certainly can keep working even after we've kicked the bucket.

For some of us, we may leave behind family members who can steward what we've left. Investing in others' lives through a non-profit organization we have a passion for can be a form of leaving a legacy, something that is bigger than ourselves, something that is lasting. We have an opportunity on this earth to contribute to as many layers as possible—ourselves, our family, our church, our community, and even those internationally—no matter the amount. This is not a dollar thing—it's a heart thing.

The five stages of the purpose continuum help illustrate how we and our finances can increase in purpose as we progress through life. Many times, our own purpose and the choices we make with our money are like a many-stranded, intertwined rope. They're tied together. Our financial actions and our why are one.

When we have financial freedom, we're free to solve problems, free to give, free to serve, free to get creative with our resources. What is holding us back? Not our finances.

SO THAT...

Sometimes unique tribulations happen in life that have a way of forming us into subject-matter experts on the very type of adversity we experience. We go through those experiences so that we can later help others going through them.

Take Marvin Charles as an example. Shortly after he was born, he was taken from his teenage mother's arms by Child Protective Services. He was raised in an abusive uncle's home and later cycled in and out of the foster care system. For years, Charles struggled with substance abuse and unsavory behavior.

When he later faced each of his own children being seized into protective custody, he reversed course and embarked on a path to rebuild his life. Years later, after proving he was a changed man, he and his newly wedded wife finally earned the right to reclaim their children. And, after going through an extraordinary process to discover who his real mother was, the very same day he got his kids back, he was reunited with his mother after 43 years of not knowing where she was. He'd been waiting on that hug his whole life. In one year's time, he was made a husband, a father, and a son.

That sort of story can transform a life, and it did for Charles. As a newly established subject-matter expert in the art of reconciling a family, he set out along with his wife, Jeanett, to start the organization Divine Alternatives for Dads Services (DADS). Together with their staff, the organization walks alongside fathers reuniting with their kids when there's been separation of any kind. He's dedicated to this work.

We can take inspiration from Charles's story of life purpose and apply it to ours. Being without his parents early in life shaped him to help solve that very same issue in others' lives. What from your past do you now have a special understanding in? What has the school of hard knocks dealt you? Even if you didn't ask for it, what ride has life taken you through that has handed you experience in an area, for better or for worse? There are things we're passionate about and things that bring us to tears. If we choose to engage in multiplying money, let's ask ourselves what cause we'd wish to financially impact. Let's focus on fueling our why—not to accumulate wealth, but to accumulate purpose.

A SUPERHERO WITH A CANE

The Bridge of Hope cares for the people of Sierra Leone, where underemployment reaches 70%, by building schools, churches, and clinics and supplying for humanitarian needs. That under-employment statistic isn't an exaggeration—70% of the working-age population of Sierra Leone lacks labor and paychecks. This likely is a stunning contrast to the socioeconomic conditions we're accustomed to. It can be eye-opening to consider ourselves citizens of the world, allowing ourselves to become involved in the well-being of anyone in need, anywhere.

Hundreds of thousands of dollars may buy a house in the U.S., but it can construct an entire middle school in Sierra Leone from the ground up. Dollars going toward this kind of cause are unquestionably supporting a legacy, as hundreds of kids attending these institutions each year learn skills they wouldn't otherwise, receive a free lunch they would likely have been without, and find hope in their futures. When schools are built within villages, children are no longer required to walk up to two hours each way along desolate roads to receive an education multiple villages away from home. That spares students the daily dangers that can come from both vehicles and strangers. No wonder the folks who started the Bridge of Hope felt an ache in their heart after recognizing this need.

As a personal passion, I've been involved with a team that creates videos for causes like the Bridge of Hope. These pieces of visual storytelling aim to dive into the heart of what a nonprofit organization does, showing who the organization helps and how lives are being transformed for the better. As we tell these stories, meeting the people in person and hearing their accounts of overcoming pain and resulting triumph is like witnessing a miracle firsthand over and over again.

Years ago, after returning from a trip to Sierra Leone to partner on one of these videos with the Bridge of Hope, I was invited to attend their annual fundraising event. There was assigned seating at the tables, and I was seated next to a tall, elderly man getting himself around with a cane, Ernie. I wondered to myself, *Is there some commonality between Ernie and me?* If so, what could that possibly be?

Well, it turned out that Ernie had covered my costs to go to Sierra Leone, and I didn't learn that until I was seated next to him. Can you imagine how my heart welled up when I realized he had done this? Offering to support me, even though he didn't even know me? He had funded the very video I traveled to create, which had a hundred hours of work invested into it.

Ernie and I became fast friends. After the event commenced and updates were shared by the ministry, the video I had been commissioned to assemble (and Ernie had funded) played onscreen. The piece shared about the need in Sierra Leone, introducing the attendees to some of the villagers who would be positively impacted by the support dollars to be raised that day.

Ernie leaned over and put his arm around me, declaring, "That's the first time I've seen that video. My wife and I drove here with a certain dollar amount in mind that we would donate today.

Don't tell her, but I just doubled it!" He said this with such glee. It was one of the purest things I've ever witnessed. He poured out such joy and elation, a level you rarely see in a person. He was a man who was stewarding some of what he had saved to sprinkle around the world and do good where he could. At his age and with his cane, he may not have been going boots-on-the-ground to Sierra Leone, but his heart sure did. He could certainly afford to send others to do so. And that he did.

A superpower can make us into a superhero. What sort of hero will you be? We have a wealth of time, talent, treasure, and thoughts to spend. What could we as people do if we were financially thriving? Our families would be supported; our giving would be more robust. We would be flourishing in our purpose, unburdened by the cost of our own survival. Maybe we could build up available assets to share like Ernie did.

NO REGRETS

I want you to be that wrinkled, balding superhero wearing a sweater with your cape, lounging in your armchair thinking about your glory days and how you took advantage of your age of superpowers during the time you had them. No regrets. You exercised your powers when they were the most potent and could do the most good. And as your powers subside some over the years, I want you to have peace with that. Subsiding powers are a part of life. Eyesight and hearing may weaken, joints may go, and, no differently, so does your multiplying power with money.

Resting in that armchair, you enjoy now knowing you and your family are covered financially, you've done what you can to avoid introducing financial strain on any of your kids or family members, and maybe, just maybe, you find yourself becoming a superhero in a new way. Your finances can now be used to help family members, a favorite cause of yours, and undertakings that can benefit others.

Giving opens up opportunity by putting us in a new lane of traffic. Think of it like a carpool lane. It's a lane where miracles occur and lives are changed on a regular basis. Driving in that lane exercises our hearts in a purposeful way and gets us to be a part of the change we want to see in the world. Saving and giving have a natural tendency to detox our system and come back to us as happiness. Maya Angelou put it this way: "I have found that among its other benefits, giving liberates the soul of the giver."

In Peter Drucker's 1954 book, *The Practice of Management,* Drucker recounts a parable of three stonecutters. All three workers are performing the same work task. Their different attitudes toward their work reflect their varying perceptions of the significance of what they are building—a cathedral. The first worker sees himself as making a living. The second sees himself as the best at his craft compared to others. The third understands he is building a cathedral that will help connect the community, provide a gathering place for people to become familiar with their Creator, and aid others in living out their purpose. In parallel, we can multiply money for our own purposes, but it may feel like it's lacking something on its own. Are we able to grow our money beyond meeting our own personal needs and put it toward the good of others? Why we are doing it, and what that why is, matters.

Conversely, we should never be afraid of losing everything we've made. We shouldn't fall in love with money to the point it becomes a burden. If we worry about losing it, having it stolen, or spending it, it can become a millstone around our necks. It's not about making money alone—it's about what we do with it.

The three financial epiphanies use our Simple Framework to show us our money-multiplying superpower.

- **Financial Epiphany #1: Doubling Years:** A single investment of money can double every 10 years.
- **Financial Epiphany #2: The Power of 16:** At the start of a 40-year career, we have the potential to multiply money by 16 times.
- **Financial Epiphany #3: Exponential Potential:** Every 10 years, our money-multiplying power reduces by half.

As our multiplying power reduces over time, we can have heart because the money we steward grows exponentially. The curves pictured on the following page illustrate that very relationship, our exponential potential, the yin and yang of saving and investing. Everybody has a turtle's race. Run it. Accept the consistent, steady process. Take heart—things move much faster later. We already know what happens to the hare.

My hope with this book is that these ideas might connect with you like they have for me. Some may pick this up and become relatively successful with their finances compared to where they were prior, some mildly so, and others not at all. But the point is to put one more perspective out there so that, in the sea of financial ideas, the epiphany I've had with money connects with the right people. I hope that will be the case for you.

Exponential Potential

Chapter Review:

From Products and Prices to People and Purpose

- **Our People-Based Why:** If we're planning on developing wealth, it's best to have our why decided up front to keep us on track. People make a great why.
- **With Great Finances Come Great Responsibility:** Multiplying money takes responsibility and self-control. Apply proper restraint.
- **A Life Lesson from Marketplace Day:** Do not simply store up money. Give, spend wisely, and enjoy life along the way.
- **The Purpose Continuum:** This explains five stages of purpose in life: Dependency, Learning, Establishing, Serving, and Legacy. Multiplying money can help us move into these latter stages beyond meeting our own needs, and it can be used to make an impact.
- **So That…:** Marvin Charles used his speckled past to find his mission in life, reconnecting fathers to their children. Has your past made you a subject-matter expert who can help people in a particular way?
- **A Superhero with a Cane:** Ernie used his finances to fund work in Sierra Leone. He became a piece of the puzzle by doing his part, investing in a cause and sending others to do work on-site.
- **No Regrets:** Apply your money-multiplying superpower in life and invest the results toward your purpose!

Action Items:

From Products and Prices to People and Purpose

- **Identify Your People-Based Why:** How would you like to provide for your family and community? Do you have a heart for seeing the youth succeed, the homeless sheltered, and the hungry fed? Do you want to make a difference in the area of education, health, or emergency relief? Identify your people-based why.
- **Causes & Nonprofit Organizations:** At charitynavigator.org, look up causes in your area. Which ones personally resonate with your interest or purpose?

APPENDIXES

The Details That Help Keep the Rest of the Book Simple

APPENDIX I

A Brief Overview of the Book

My hope is that you can use what you've read about in this book to alter your financial life for the better. The following is a quick summary of the chapters to review what you've learned and help you put it to use.

Chapter 1
Preparing Ourselves to Think Differently

William Kamkambwa's story introduced to us the four steps of experiencing an epiphany: Seeking a Solution, The Struggle, Coming to a Realization, and Taking Action.

STEP 1: SEEKING A SOLUTION

Chapter 2
You're Not an Impostor—This Is Possible

Ronald Read, our millionaire janitor, proved to us that great wealth is attainable regardless of income. This is for you. Just get started.

STEP 2: THE STRUGGLE

Chapter 3
What's Stopping Us from Having an Epiphany?

The six financial mental blocks act as barriers that prevent us from having an epiphany over our money. These blocks are debt, financial crises, analysis paralysis, fear/trust/risk, keeping up with the Joneses, and lifestyle inflation. We must escape the grasp of each one.

STEP 3: COMING TO A REALIZATION

Chapter 4
First Comes the Framework

The three principles that create our Simple Framework are starting work at age 22, working for 40 years, and earning a 7.2% rate of return on invested money.

Chapter 5
Financial Epiphany #1: Doubling Years

A single investment can double every 10 years when invested with the Simple Framework in mind.

Chapter 6
Financial Epiphany #2: The Power of 16

When we start our careers, we have the multiplying power of 16 with money invested at that time.

Chapter 7
Financial Epiphany #3: Exponential Potential

Every 10 years, our money-multiplying power reduces by half. Understanding this helps quantify what is happening to our multiplying power over time.

STEP 4: TAKING ACTION

Chapter 8
Let's Set Up Your Money-Multiplying Machine

401(k) plans, IRAs, and brokerage accounts are capable of holding assets that are suitable for multiplying money.

Chapter 9
Unleashing Our Exponential Potential

There are various financial offensive moves we can implement in each decade of life to optimize our finances.

Chapter 10
Strategic Moves for the Newly Inspired

We can apply our money-multiplying superpower to a college fund, custodial account, or forever fund.

Chapter 11
From Products and Prices to People and Purpose

The purpose continuum has five stages: Dependency, Learning, Establishing, Serving, and Legacy. We can place a purpose on our money beyond serving ourselves once our own needs are met.

APPENDIX II

A Peek Under the Hood

The next pages are intentionally left outside of the core of this book for one good reason: they saunter outside the boundaries of simple! The whole purpose of this book is to empower us with an understanding of our money-multiplying superpower, simply stated, using stories and analogies when possible. And, as a result, maybe that knowledge will inspire us to stay out of debt, invest, and put those multiplied funds toward good. But for those curious to see more of what is running under the hood, let's take a look.

THE RULE OF 72

As I began my journey of learning personal finance, the rule of 72 became one of the rules of thumb that pricked me and woke me from my financial slumber. It's a simplified way to determine how long an investment will take to double, given a fixed annual rate of return. By dividing the number 72 by the annual rate of return, investors can get a rough estimate of how many years it will take for an initial investment to duplicate itself.

> The Number 72 ÷ Rate of Return = Years to Double the Initial Investment
>
> So, by plugging in a rate of return, in our case 7.2%, we get…
>
> 72 ÷ 7.2 = 10 years to double the initial investment

This means that an investment with a 7.2% rate of return will double in 10 years.

We use this particular set of numbers, out of all the possibilities, because 7.2% is a normal rate of return when investing and 10 years is an easy number to calculate and do mental math with.

Say we'd like to use the rule of 72 to figure out how other rates of return would result in different doubling years.

> 72 ÷ Rate of Return = Years to Double the Initial Investment
> 72 ÷ 10 = 7.2 years
> 72 ÷ 9 = 8 years
> 72 ÷ 8 = 9 years
> 72 ÷ 7 = 10.3 years
> 72 ÷ 6 = 12 years
> 72 ÷ 5 = 14.4 years
> 72 ÷ 4 = 18 years
> 72 ÷ 3 = 24 years

Even though these are approximations using a rule of thumb, the results tell an important story, which is the effect that the rate of return has on doubling an initial investment. The table on the following page takes these results and compares them side by side with the results of a more complex—but accurate—calculation for rate of return.

Comparing the Rule of 72 with a Detailed Calculation

Rate of Return	Doubling Years (using the rule of 72)	Doubling Years (using detailed calculation)
10%	7.2 years	7.27 years
9%	8 years	8.04 years
8%	9 years	9.01 years
7%	10.3 years	10.24 years
6%	12 years	11.90 years
5%	14.4 years	14.21 years
4%	18 years	17.67 years
3%	24 years	23.45 years

The next graph shows our typical 7.2% interest rate and the doubling of a single $1 investment over 40 years. But what if we experience a rough market or are more conservative with our investing? Or what if the market goes on a tear and we garner larger returns than expected? See the scenarios on the following page that vary from a 4% return all the way up to a 10% return. Once again, 7.2% allows for easy math (those numbers are rounded for further simplicity). But we can see the significant difference the rate of return makes when multiplying money.

Multiplying Money with Different Rates of Return

		10 yrs	20 yrs	30 yrs	40 yrs
4%	$1	$1.48	$2.19	$3.24	$4.80
5%	$1	$1.63	$2.65	$4.32	$7.04
6%	$1	$1.79	$3.21	$5.74	$10.29
7.2%	$1	$2	$4	$8	$16
8%	$1	$2.16	$4.66	$10.06	$21.72
9%	$1	$2.37	$5.60	$13.27	$31.41
10%	$1	$2.59	$6.73	$17.45	$45.26

Now, if we take the top three lines listed in this table and graph them, we come up with the curves on the following pages.[24] See how 6%, 5%, and 4% rates of return lay out different multiplying powers over the typical four decades of work.

[24] These graphs are for illustrative purposes only and do not demonstrate scale or a relationship relative to one another.

Multiplying Power: 6% Rate of Return

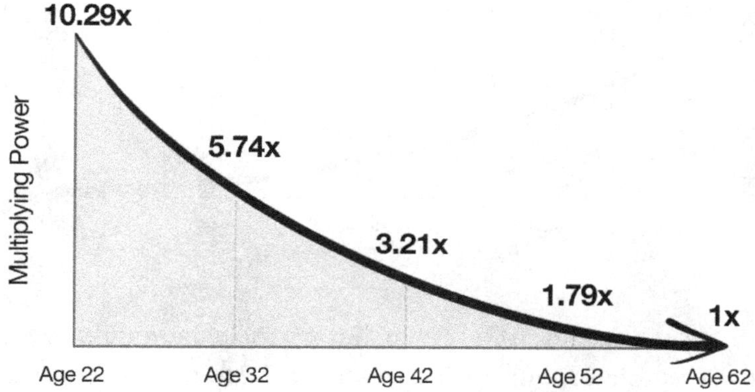

Multiplying Power: 5% Rate of Return

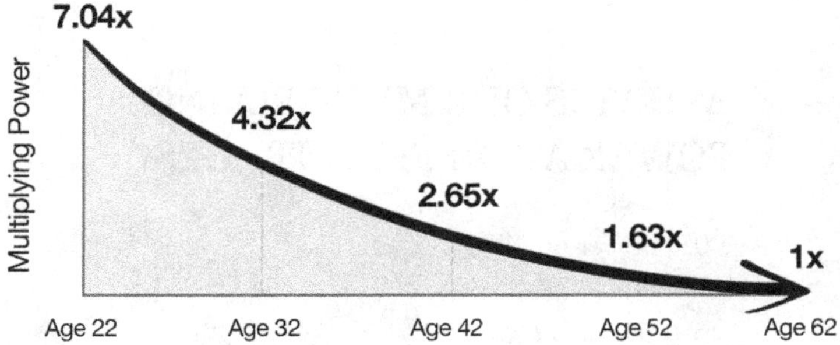

Multiplying Power: 4% Rate of Return

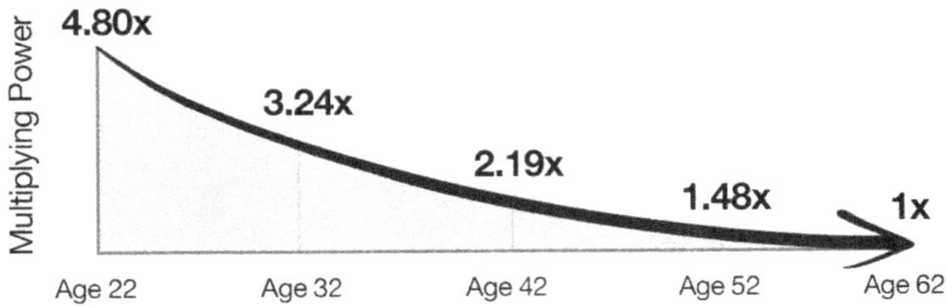

For the ages in the following list, see the money-multiplying power associated with each age when a 7.2% rate of return is maintained and the money is left invested until age 62. The ages and numbers in bold are the ones that are approximated and referred to in this book: the power of 64 at age 2, the power of 32 at age 12, the power of 16 at age 22, the power of 8 at age 32, the power of 4 at 42, the power of 2 at 52, and spending down investments at age 62.

WHAT IS OUR MULTIPLYING POWER AT DIFFERENT AGES?

Age 0 = Power of 74.49
Age 1 = Power of 69.48
Age 2 = Power of 64.82
Age 3 = Power of 60.46
Age 4 = Power of 56.40
Age 5 = Power of 52.61
Age 6 = Power of 49.08
Age 7 = Power of 45.78
Age 8 = Power of 42.71

Age 9 = Power of 39.84
Age 10 = Power of 37.16
Age 11 = Power of 34.67
Age 12 = Power of 32.34
Age 13 = Power of 30.17
Age 14 = Power of 28.14
Age 15 = Power of 26.25
Age 16 = Power of 24.49
Age 17 = Power of 22.84
Age 18 = Power of 21.31
Age 19 = Power of 19.88
Age 20 = Power of 18.54
Age 21 = Power of 17.30
Age 22 = Power of 16.14
Age 23 = Power of 15.05
Age 24 = Power of 14.04
Age 25 = Power of 13.10
Age 26 = Power of 12.22
Age 27 = Power of 11.40
Age 28 = Power of 10.63
Age 29 = Power of 9.92
Age 30 = Power of 9.25
Age 31 = Power of 8.63
Age 32 = Power of 8.05
Age 33 = Power of 7.51
Age 34 = Power of 7.01
Age 35 = Power of 6.54
Age 36 = Power of 6.10
Age 37 = Power of 5.69
Age 38 = Power of 5.30
Age 39 = Power of 4.95
Age 40 = Power of 4.62

Age 41 = Power of 4.31
Age 42 = Power of 4.02
Age 43 = Power of 3.75
Age 44 = Power of 3.50
Age 45 = Power of 3.26
Age 46 = Power of 3.04
Age 47 = Power of 2.84
Age 48 = Power of 2.65
Age 49 = Power of 2.47
Age 50 = Power of 2.30
Age 51 = Power of 2.15
Age 52 = Power of 2.00
Age 53 = Power of 1.87
Age 54 = Power of 1.74
Age 55 = Power of 1.63
Age 56 = Power of 1.52
Age 57 = Power of 1.42
Age 58 = Power of 1.32
Age 59 = Power of 1.23
Age 60 = Power of 1.15
Age 61 = Power of 1.07
Age 62 = Power of 1.00

WHAT IF I RETIRE EARLY?

The numbers can shift if you plan on retiring early. These, of course, are guidelines to help us plan and take action. The real world will send us some curveballs. But if you retire at 52, your multiplying power could look like the following:

Age 22 = Power of 8
Age 32 = Power of 4

Age 42 = Power of 2
Age 52 = Power of 1

WHAT IF I WORK LONGER?

You can shift the numbers if you choose to work longer in life. For example, if you work to the age of 72, your multiplying power would look like the following:

Age 22 = Power of 32
Age 32 = Power of 16
Age 42 = Power of 8
Age 52 = Power of 4
Age 62 = Power of 2
Age 72 = Power of 1

Once again, these are guidelines, and investing will have its ups and downs along the way. Always confide in your financial advisor to see how best to adjust your saved resources to preserve and continue to multiply portions and eventually spend from.

WILL THE RATE OF RETURN VARY OVER MY LIFETIME?

The rate of return on our investments will fluctuate. Rising markets may temporarily lift our rate of return multiple times over what we expect, and declining markets may temporarily pull back a large percentage on the value of what we own. It's all part of the roller coaster the financial markets ride. But history tells us that the market has steadily moved upward over long periods of time. Retirement expert Chris Hogan pointedly remarks that we shouldn't get off the roller coaster in the midst of riding it. This wisdom indicates that we should stick things out and have a plan for disembarking when the journey is over for our careers.

Many financial advisors will recommend that we have a more aggressive mix of investments when we are younger. That gives us a chance of capturing a higher rate of return while we can take on more risk. Most will suggest adjusting to be more conservative with our investments five or more years before our target retirement date.

The rationale in choosing to invest in assets that potentially lower our rate of return before retirement is to reduce the impact of market volatility on our retirement nest egg, as we have less time to recover from any significant downturns. With less risk typically comes less return. By transitioning to more conservative investments, such as bonds or cash equivalents, we aim to preserve the capital we've accumulated.

How Do Different Rates of Return Impact When We Have the Power of 16?

Rate of Return	Multiplying Power	Years of Investing
4%	Power of 16	71 years
5%	Power of 16	57 years
6%	Power of 16	48 years
7.2%	Power of 16	40 years
8%	Power of 16	36 years
9%	Power of 16	32 years
10%	Power of 16	29 years

At the rates listed on the previous page, we would wield the money-multiplying power of 16 by investing for approximately the number of years listed. When maintaining a 7.2% rate of return, we have the power of 16 by investing for approximately 40 years.

WHAT OTHER VARIABLES ARE THERE TO CONSIDER WHEN INVESTING?

Many investments require us to pay fees to the people and companies managing our money. Choosing high-quality investments with low fees is a good approach to take so that fees have a minimal effect on our returns each year. Warren Buffett, perhaps the world's most renowned investor, recommends investing in an index fund that tracks the S&P 500.[25]

For investments that pay out dividends, reinvesting those dividends is recommended and can accelerate the multiplying of our funds. Some employers may opt to match employee contributions to retirement plans. That can give a nice boost to the money injected into a retirement account from the beginning. As we've stated throughout the book, another variable to keep in mind is inflation—and the impact it may have on our spending power over the long run. And don't forget how taxes will play into things.

The average person in the workforce labors 40 years to support a retirement of up to 30 years. In a way, every year we work, we're saving up for nine months of retirement life too. That's a

---

25 The Standard & Poor's 500 is a stock market index that measures the performance of 500 of the largest publicly traded companies in the United States. It is a key indicator of the overall condition of the U.S. stock market and is one of the most widely followed stock indices. Ask a financial advisor if a market capitalization–based fund or an equally weighted fund might be a good fit for you.

lot to be responsible for! With advances in medicine, we're living longer than ever. And with the ever-growing expense of health care, including long-term care costs, having prepared well for retirement can bring more peace than ever. What if we don't feel we have enough saved up for retirement? We can always choose to work longer or spend less over those years. Does it matter if we have $1 million saved versus $1.5 million, or even $500k? The idea of this book is not so much the final amount that we save but that we understand multiplying money so we can be empowered to take confident action.

BIBLIOGRAPHY

CHAPTER 1

Ejiofor, Chiwetel, dir. *The Boy Who Harnessed The Wind* 2019; BBC Films, Netflix.

Yamamura, George. *The 10th Inning.* Self-published, G. Yamamura. 2005.

CHAPTER 2

Anderer, John. "Survey: The Average Person Will Watch More Than 78,000 Hours of TV." 2019. https://studyfinds.org/survey-the-average-adult-will-watch-more-than-78000-hours-of-tv/.

CHAPTER 3

"Advertising Spending in Selected Markets Worldwide in 2024." Statista. May 17, 2024. https://www.statista.com/forecasts/1380173/ad-spending-markets-worldwide.

"Advertising Spending Per Capita in the United States from 2020 to 2022." Statista. November 15, 2023. https://www.statista.com/statistics/309732/ad-spend-per-person-usa.

Appleby, Chloe. "How Many People Have Student Loan Debt?" BestColleges. Last updated January 19, 2024. https://www.bestcolleges.com/research/how-many-people-have-student-loans.

"At a Glance: Tackling Student Loan Debt." College Affordability Act. Accessed June 10, 2024. https://democrats-edworkforce.house.gov/imo/media/doc/CAA%20At%20A%20Glance%20--%20LOANS%20.pdf.

Brown, Natalia. "How to Pay Off Credit Card Debt With a Low Income." National Debt Relief. June 14, 2022. https://www.nationaldebtrelief.com/blog/debt-guide/credit-card-debt/how-to-pay-off-credit-card-debt-with-low-income-ndr/.

Cherry, Kendra. "The Asch Conformity Experiments." Verywell Mind. Last updated November 13, 2023. https://www.verywellmind.com/the-asch-conformity-experiments-2794996.

De Visé, Daniel. " 'The Least Affordable Housing Market in Recent Memory': Why Now Is a Great Time to Rent." USA Today. Last updated February 26, 2024. https://www.usatoday.com/story/money/2024/02/16/housing-market-favors-rent-vs-buy/72599444007.

Dickler, Jessica. "60% of Americans Are Still Living Paycheck to Paycheck as Inflation Hits Workers' Wages." CNBC. September 27, 2023. https://www.cnbc.com/2023/09/27/60percent-of-americans-are-still-living-paycheck-to-paycheck.html.

Fay, Bill. "How to Avoid Going into Debt for a Wedding." Debt.

org. Last updated March 24, 2023. https://www.debt.org/family/wedding/.

Garg, Amit. "Reinventing Credit Cards: Responses to New Lending Models in the US." McKinsey & Company. June 23, 2022. https://www.mckinsey.com/industries/financial-services/our-insights/reinventing-credit-cards-responses-to-new-lending-models-in-the-us#/.

Holtz, Allan. *American Newspaper Comics: An Encyclopedic Reference Guide*. Ann Arbor: The University of Michigan Press, 2012.

Housel, Morgan. *The Psychology of Money*. Petersfield, UK: Harriman House, 2020.

"How Much Does the Average Person Make in a Lifetime?" Zippia. January 7, 2023. https://www.zippia.com/answers/how-much-does-the-average-person-make-in-a-lifetime.

Leonhardt, Megan. "Americans Spend Over $1,000 a Year on Lotto Tickets." CNBC. December 12, 2019. https://www.cnbc.com/2019/12/12/americans-spend-over-1000-dollars-a-year-on-lotto-tickets.html.

Li, Yun. "Warren Buffett Says 'Never Bet Against America' in Letter Trumpeting Berkshire's U.S.-Based Assets." CNBC. Last updated March 1, 2021. https://www.cnbc.com/2021/02/27/warren-buffett-says-never-bet-against-america-in-letter-trumpeting-berkshires-us-based-assets.html.

Luthi, Ben, Andrew Pentis and Katie Lowery. "What Is the Average Student Loan Debt in 2024 — And What Are the Impacts?" CNN, January 23, 2024, https://www.cnn.com/cnn-underscored/money/average-student-loan-debt.

Peppercorn, Susan. "Why You Should Stop Trying to Be Happy

at Work." *Harvard Business Review*. July 26, 2019. https://hbr.org/2019/07/why-you-should-stop-trying-to-be-happy-at-work.

Pokora, Becky. "Credit Card Statistics and Trends 2024." *Forbes*. Last updated March 28, 2024, https://www.forbes.com/advisor/credit-cards/credit-card-statistics.

"Report on the Economic Well-Being of U.S. Households in 2022 - May 2023." Federal Reserve. Last updated June 2, 2023. https://www.federalreserve.gov/publications/2023-economic-well-being-of-us-households-in-2022-expenses.htm.

Robin, Vicki and Joe Dominguez. *Your Money or Your Life*. New York: Penguin Books, 2018.

Williams, H.K. "The Group Plan." *The Biblical World* 53, no. 1 (1919): 80–81.

Wood, Sarah. "How Much Student Loan Debt Does the Average College Graduate Have?" U.S. News and World Report. September 22, 2023. https://www.usnews.com/education/best-colleges/paying-for-college/articles/see-how-student-loan-borrowing-has-changed.

CHAPTER 4

"Erno Rubik: Hungarian Inventor." *Encyclopedia Britannica*. Last updated December 13, 2023. https://www.britannica.com/biography/Erno-Rubik.

Gonzalez, Robbie. "How to Solve a Rubik's Cube." *WIRED*. September 5, 2019. https://www.wired.com/story/how-to-solve-a-rubiks-cube-step-by-step.

CHAPTER 5

Baldridge, Rebecca. "The Rule of 72: How It Works and Why It Matters." *Forbes*. Last updated April 10, 2023. https://www.forbes.com/advisor/investing/rule-of-72.

Banton, Caroline. "The Rule of 72: What It Is and How to Use It in Investing." Investopedia. Last updated December 11, 2023. https://www.investopedia.com/ask/answers/what-is-the-rule-72.

Grant, Adam. *Originals*. New York: Penguin Books, 2017.

Mischel, Walter. *The Marshmallow Test*. New York: Hachette Book Group, 2014.

Newman, Cathy. "How 'Eureka' Moments in Science Happen." National Geographic. May 23, 2017. https://www.nationalgeographic.com/science/article/eureka-insight-newton-archimedes-genius-science.

Young, Roger. "You're Age 35, 50, or 60: How Much Should You Have Saved for Retirement by Now?" T. Rowe Price. May 29, 2024. https://www.troweprice.com/personal-investing/resources/insights/youre-age-35-50-or-60-how-much-should-you-have-by-now.html.

CHAPTER 6

Bloom, Leslie. "How Long Is the Average Career of an NFL Player?" Chron. Last updated March 5, 2019. https://work.chron.com/long-average-career-nfl-player-12643.html.

Lupkin, Sydney. "Too Old to Be an Olympic Figure Skater? There's Always Curling." ABC News. February 12, 2014.

https://abcnews.go.com/blogs/health/2014/02/12/too-old-to-be-an-olympic-figure-skater-theres-always-curling.

Ziebelman, Alexis. "Peaking at 16: The Reality of Penn's Female Gymnasts." *The Daily Pennsylvanian*. March 13, 2013. https://www.thedp.com/article/2013/03/peaking-at-16-the-reality-of-female-gymnasts.

CHAPTER 7

Brown, H. Jackson. *P.S. I Love You*. Nashville: Rutledge Hill Press, 1990.

Chesterton, Gilbert Keith. *Tremendous Trifles*. New York: Dodd, Mead and Company, 1909.

Colomer, Nora. "Most Seniors Regret Retirement Planning Decisions, Want Do-Over: Survey." Fox Business. July 11, 2023. https://www.foxbusiness.com/personal-finance/seniors-regret-not-saving-earlier.

"Exponential Growth & Decay: FAQ." Khan Academy. Accessed June 10, 2024. https://www.khanacademy.org/math/algebra/x2f8bb11595b61c86:exponential-growth-decay/x2f8bb11595b61c86:exponential-vs-linear-models/a/exponential-growth-decay-faq.

Poldrack, Russell. "What Is Loss Aversion?" *Scientific American*. July 1, 2016. https://www.scientificamerican.com/article/what-is-loss-aversion/.

CHAPTER 8

Hartman, Rachel and Emily Brandon. "Nine Jobs That Still Offer Traditional Pensions." U.S. News and World Report. January 11, 2024. https://money.usnews.com/money/retirement/baby-boomers/articles/jobs-that-still-offer-traditional-pensions.

Smith, Jacquelyn. "Steve Jobs Always Dressed Exactly the Same. Here's Who Else Does." *Forbes.* October 5, 2012. https://www.forbes.com/sites/jacquelynsmith/2012/10/05/steve-jobs-always-dressed-exactly-the-same-heres-who-else-does.

CHAPTER 9

Stevens, Janet. *The Tortoise and the Hare: An Aesop Fable.* New York: Holiday House, 1984.

CHAPTER 10

Investment Calculator. Calculator.net. Accessed June 10, 2024. https://www.calculator.net/investment-calculator.html.

Maxwell, John C. (TheJohnCMaxwell). "Remember, a budget is telling your money where to go instead of wondering where it went. - John Maxwell #JMTeam." Twitter. February 11, 2016. https://x.com/TheJohnCMaxwell/status/697827645896192000.

Stanley, Thomas J., and Sarah Stanley Fallaw. *The Next Millionaire Next Door.* Guilford, CT: Lyons Press, 2019.

Tuchman, Mitch. "Opinion: Kevin O'Leary: This Easy Math Trick Helps You Crush Retirement Goals." MarketWatch.

August 27, 2019. https://www.marketwatch.com/story/kevin-oleary-this-easy-math-trick-helps-you-crush-retirement-goals-2019-03-28.

CHAPTER 11

"An African Development Bank Project Is Creating Skills and New Jobs for the Youth in Sierra Leone." African Development Bank Group. February 1, 2023. https://www.afdb.org/en/success-stories/african-development-bank-project-creating-skills-and-new-jobs-youth-sierra-leone-58695.

Angelou, Maya. *Wouldn't Take Nothing for My Journey Now*. New York: Random House, 1993.

Drucker, Eric. *The Practice of Management*. New York: Harper & Row, 1954.

Lagatta, Eric. "Lotto Regret: Pitfalls of Powerball, Lottery Winners Serve as Cautionary Tales as Jackpots Swell." USA Today. Last updated July 20, 2023. https://www.usatoday.com/story/news/nation/2023/07/19/powerball-mega-millions-winners-instant-billionaire-regrets/70430571007.

Staley, Oliver. "Warren Buffett Says He Simply Had the Good Luck of Winning the 'Ovarian Lottery' To Be Born American." Quartz. January 30, 2017. https://qz.com/898048/trumps-immigrant-travel-ban-warren-buffett-reminds-americans-that-they-simply-had-the-good-luck-of-winning-the-ovarian-lottery-to-be-born-in-the-us.

"Where We Serve: Sierra Leone." Bridge of Hope. Accessed June 14, 2024. https://www.thebridgeofhope.us/where-we-serve#sierra-leone.

Wing, Jennifer, and Kevin Kniestedt. "One Man's Journey Through Drugs, Recovery, Getting His Family Back and Paying It Forward." KNKX Public Radio. September 16, 2017. https://www.knkx.org/other-news/2017-09-16/one-mans-journey-through-drugs-recovery-getting-his-family-back-and-paying-it-forward.

APPENDIX

Ganguly, Aditi. "Warren Buffett Believes In S&P 500 Index Funds - But Are They Really Worth It?" Yahoo Finance. May 14, 2024. https://finance.yahoo.com/news/warren-buffett-believes-p-500-170220804.html.

Hogan, Chris. *Everyday Millionaires.* Ramsey Press, The Lampo Group, LLC, 2019.

THANKS TO

Thanks to my family for the support, including lending me an endless ear and being part of the first round of readers: Su Yamamura, Logan Yamamura, Linda Sakamoto, Michael Symphony, and Raven Otero-Symphony. Thanks to my dad, George Yamamura, for training me to look at the world differently in the way that you did.

Thank you to my mentors, including Keith Ferrin for inspiring me with your bold way of communicating and for running me through your book workshop, Doug Humphreys for providing guidance in my faith and demonstrating what emotional intelligence looks like, and Diane Tieskie for showing me how to value others.

Thank you to my career sponsors, advocates, and mentors: Sue McConnaha, Sandy Torrey, Amy Walker, Lorri Curry, Robb Walters, and Linda Castillo. And thank you to my team, Emma Blauser, Gordon Jacobson and Allan Fitzgerald. We're training to be master communicators. We never expect to reach that goal, but we're always trying.

Thanks to my friends and coworkers, Brooke Perry and Ally van Ingen, for being intentional and joining in serving together. Thanks to Joe Pham for being a financially savvy colleague to bounce ideas off of. Thanks to Lynn Cruz and Derek Berndt for demonstrating service in the workplace to me. Thanks to Mike Dorpat for showing me how to be strategic with giving through leveraging company matching to give to the church.

Thanks to Matt Worthington and Jamie Gu for sharing your expertise and perspective as professionals in the financial industry.

Thanks to Chris Lauri, James Starlin, Josh Allred, Paul Gwinnup Jr., and the Created To Create team for your hearts and for using your passion for creating to serve God.

Thank you to Matthew Chi, Johnny Lin, and Kelly Humphreys for your encouragement and insights as I proceeded with this book.

Thank you to Marvin and Jeanett Charles from DADS, Geri Jeffery from the Bridge of Hope, and Michelle Frets from Vine Maple Place for making a difference in so many people's lives with your ministries and showing me how our purpose and our why can be lived out.

Thank you to Financial Peace University and Crossroads Bible Church for sparking my interest in finances and for making personal finance simple and empowering to learn.

Thank you to Mr. Eyman for looking out for me, encouraging me, and challenging me with opportunities in your Speech class.

Thank you to William and Olivia Scott Kamkwamba for inspiring me and others with what you are doing at Moving Windmills. And thank you to Gemma May Kimani for helping facilitate the inclusion of William's story in this book.

And thank you to the Book Launchers team for guiding me through this process, refining the work, and taking the book from manuscript to final printed piece!

CAUSES WRITTEN ABOUT IN THIS BOOK

WILLIAM KAMKWAMBA AND MOVING WINDMILLS

William Kamkwamba, originating from Kasungu, Malawi, embodies resilience and innovation. Facing a devastating famine and forced to leave school, he embraced self-education, stumbling upon a windmill image in a library book. Using scrapyard pieces—a broken bicycle, a tractor fan, and more—he crafted windmills that symbolized hope for his community, providing them with electricity and water.

To navigate challenges like Kamkwamba's, resilient problem-solvers are needed—beginning with an education reflecting Malawi's reality, focusing on securing livelihoods through improved agriculture. The Moving Windmills Project, inspired by Kamkwamba, aims to cultivate innovators worldwide. Evolving since 2008, the project has shifted focus to community resource centers, empowering thousands with sustainable resources, education, and opportunities. With a team and global partners, Moving Windmills fosters cross-border collaborations, uniting communities for impactful and lasting change. Moving Windmills invites all to join in on their transformative journey.

MARVIN CHARLES AND DADS

In 1998, Marvin and Jeanett Charles faced addiction, poverty, and spiritual emptiness, with four children in the Child Protective Services system. Their lives took a transformative turn when Marvin Charles experienced a spiritual awakening, praying for family reunification. God had a bigger plan that not only included Charles's immediate family, but, unexpectedly, also involved Charles's reunion with his long-lost parents, rekindling their relationship.

Motivated by their journey, the Charles family established the nonprofit Divine Alternatives for Dads Services (DADS), which is dedicated to giving fathers hope by providing support and navigating relational and legal barriers to reconnect with their children. In a recent year, DADS assisted 435 fathers, impacted 1,192 children, and successfully graduated 51 fathers from the DADS 13-week "Becoming DADS" parenting classes. DADS has provided services to over 5,000 fathers, serving the community from its head office in Seattle, Washington.

THE BRIDGE OF HOPE

The Bridge of Hope aims to help make Sierra Leone a place where its people have access to the basic needs of life, where they are healthy, equipped, and empowered to support themselves and find purpose in serving others. Foundational to the work of this organization is the belief that to change the world, we must take a holistic approach, one that focuses on the proclamation of the gospel and meeting physical needs such as needs for health care, food, clean water, and education.

The team strives to walk alongside the people of Sierra Leone to partner with them in building community and hope. In addition, the ministry believes that, while doing this, lives are changed on both sides of "the bridge." The Bridge of Hope is headquartered in Maple Valley, Washington.

PRAISE FOR *FINANCIAL EPIPHANY*

Financial Epiphany contains key personal finance lessons that are simplified and easy to understand. Scott infuses his book with anecdotes and personal stories that make learnings relatable and easy to absorb. We all need to utilize our money-multiplying superpower to help guide us on our path to financial well-being.

— Matthew Chi
Vice President of Finance

Every parent attending a college graduation ceremony needs to bring their graduate this book as a gift for their financial future.

— Jamie Gu
Financial Advisor/Executive Director

This book is an essential read for those who have yet to realize their money-multiplying superpower. We all have it, but the earlier in life we start saving money, the more we unleash exponential growth with those funds.

— Joe Pham
Founder, Financial Fitness Club

Many of us are weighed down by concerns and unknowns when it comes to finances. This reality not only impacts our pocketbook but our families, other relationships, and even our spiritual and mental health. *Financial Epiphany* provides a lifeline that not only provides hope but a plan for moving from financial fear to financial freedom.

— **Doug Humphreys**
Former Attorney, Director, and Pastor

Experiencing financial epiphanies is possible with the steps Scott clearly lays out, and the parables he teaches with are inspiring examples. Exactly what first-time students of finances need to hear.

— **Alexandra van Ingen**
Corporate Content Specialist

What Scott has created in *Financial Epiphany* is equal parts simple, practical, and transformational. It's simple enough to understand. It's practical enough to actually put into practice. And it will be transformational for decades to come. Read it…and put Scott's wisdom into practice. You—and your kids and grandkids—will be glad you did!

— **Keith Ferrin**
Author and Speaker, keithferrin.com

We're all tempted to make purchases to secure short bouts of happiness. This book teaches that we can nudge ourselves away from solely buying things of limited value and turn our money toward things of limitless value—serving each other and making the world a better place.

— **Brooke Perry**
Manager of Community Relations and Giving Campaigns

Download the *Financial Epiphany* Money Moves Guide

What's next? Don't stop. Keep the momentum going. Continue to empower yourself by learning about the practical topics and money moves below:

Making Your First Investment

Deleting Debt

Meeting with a Financial Professional

Deciding How Much to Save for Retirement

These topics are covered in the *Financial Epiphany* Money Moves guide. Download the guide at

financialepiphany.com/moneymoves.

So Go & Multiply

We have an opportunity to empower others with the money they manage. Spreading this simple message of financial understanding and empowerment can help others on the road to reaching their own financial epiphanies and their own financial best. Below are some opportunities for us to work together. Let's get in touch.

For discounted bulk purchases of this book for your company, association, or conference, please email:

scott@financialepiphany.com.

For more resources, or to book Scott for interviews or speaking, visit:

financialepiphany.com

Thank you for reading!

If you enjoyed *Financial Epiphany*, please leave a review on Goodreads or on the retailer site where you purchased this book.

www.ingramcontent.com/pod-product-compliance
Lightning Source LLC
LaVergne TN
LVHW091054131224
798987LV00001B/1
9798991385701